THE NATIONAL HEALTH
or
NURSE NORTON'S AFFAIR

By the same author

JOE EGG

The National Health

or

Nurse Norton's Affair

A play in two acts
by
PETER NICHOLS

Grove Press, Inc., New York

ISBN: 0-394-17836-X
Grove Press ISBN: 0-8021-0080-5

Library of Congress Catalog Card Number: 74-24861

First Evergreen Edition

Manufactured in the United States of America

Distributed by Random House, Inc.

GROVE PRESS, INC., 53 East 11th Street,
New York, New York 10003

The first production of *The National Health* was given at the National Theatre on 16 October 1969. The cast was as follows:

Patients	REES	Gerald James
	TYLER	Patrick Carter
	ASH	Robert Lang
	FOSTER	Bernard Gallagher
	KEN	John Nightingale
	FLAGG	Harry Lomax
	LOACH	Charles Kay
	MACKIE	Brian Oulton
Nursing staff	MATRON	Mary Griffiths
	SISTER MCPHEE	Maggie Riley
	STAFF NURSE NORTON	Cleo Sylvestre
	NURSE SWEET	Anna Carteret
	NURSE LAKE	Isabelle Lucas
	ORIENTAL NURSE	Helen Fleming
	BARNET	Jim Dale
	MICHAEL	John Flint
	PRINCE	John Hamilton
Doctors	MR. BOYD	Paul Curran
	NEIL, HIS SON	Robert Walker
	DR. BIRD	Gillian Barge
	INDIAN STUDENT	Malcolm Reid
	OLD WOMAN	Gabrielle Laye
	CHAPLAIN	George Browne

Theatre staff, other visitors, etc Tom Baker, Frederick Bennett, Jean Boht, Michael Edgar, Roger Forbes, Michael Harding, Norma Streader

7

Musicians   Jack Botterell, Laurie Morgan, Norman
Wells, Rod Wilmott

PRODUCTION BY	Michael Blakemore
DESIGNED BY	Patrick Robertson
LIGHTING BY	Robert Bryan
MUSIC BY	Marc Wilkinson

ACT ONE

Scene One

The first arrivals find the stage lit dimly by a blue bulb hanging centre, but during the next fifteen minutes a steadily increasing dawn light reveals one end of a hospital ward.

This daylight creeps through Victorian Gothic windows high in the rear wall. Above eight feet, the walls are pea-green, below this white. Against the back wall are five beds, with a locker between each and earphones and thermometers in wall brackets. The ward is supposed to continue off to the audience's left and there is no side-wall, only masking flats. The wall on the right is the end of the ward and an open way leads to Sister's room, kitchen, lavatories and the main corridor. The wall continues diagonally downstage and here is one more bed, called 6. Halfway down on the audience's left is a large black coke stove with a chimney rising from it and going out of sight into the flies. Armchairs are grouped around it.

From the apron on the stage, two flights of steps go down into the orchestra pit. Between them at the bottom is a cinema organ or piano, if the production is to use music.

The directions refer to the beds by numbers from left to right. Each one has a male patient in it, except Bed 3, which is made but empty.

CLEO NORTON, a West Indian Staff Nurse, crosses the stage from time to time while the audience is assembling. She sometimes checks a patient, giving special attention to the man in Bed 5, who is being drip-fed and drained. From the other patients come groans, snores and incoherent utterances. Sometimes we can hear what they say.

ASH (*bed 1*): No . . . no . . . please don't do that . . .
    (*Someone groans at this, then snores as before. After a long*

9

time, a shout):

REES (*bed 4*): Take your bloody hands off me!

(*Several groans. Then snores, as before. A dawn chorus of city birds is heard as the light increases.*

ASH sits up, looks at REES, climbs out of bed, scratches his head, looks at his wristwatch. He gets a dressing-gown from his locker, puts it on: then slippers. Sitting on his bed, he looks into a hand mirror at the condition of his tongue.

TYLER pushes on from the left in a wheelchair. We should notice that his legs have been amputated at the knee.)

TYLER (*loud and hearty*): Morning!

ASH: Oh—good morning to you, sir.

TYLER: Lovely morning.

ASH: We'll live in hopes——

TYLER: Beautiful!

ASH: —if we die in despair . . .

(*TYLER has gone on off right. We hear him continuing as ASH rummages in his locker.*)

TYLER (*off*): Morning, Staff Nurse.

STAFF (*off*): Morning, Mister Tyler.

TYLER (*off*): Lovely morning.

STAFF (*off*): Looks it.

TYLER: (*off*): Beautiful!

(*FOSTER (Bed 2) has been woken by TYLER's reveille. Props himself on an elbow, scratches head. ASH has his towel and shaving bag.*)

FOSTER: Morning.

ASH: Good morning to you, friend.

FOSTER: He likes to make a row.

ASH: Who's that?

FOSTER: Whosit—just been through——

ASH: Tyler.

FOSTER: What a voice.

ASH: Wonderful spirit, though, considering——

FOSTER: Oh, yes.

10

(ASH *stands, checking his gear.* FOSTER *glances round,*
sees that Bed 3 is empty.)
Where's Mister Lucas then?

ASH : Of course, you didn't hear. You get a wonderful sleep.

FOSTER : I do, yes.

ASH : Very enviable. He went in the night.

FOSTER : In that condition? Never. Transferred?

ASH : (*quietly*) : Passed on. First I knew was the screens going
round then the resuscitation unit and the heart-machine
. . . quite a pantomime but . . . n.b.g. . . . I regret to
say. . . .

FOSTER : I'm blowed.

ASH : The orderly cleaned him and wheeled him off . . .

FOSTER : I suppose it was a blessing.

ASH : A happy release, yes. I must find myself a basin before
the headlong rush of the Gadarene swine.
(FOSTER *nods and* ASH *goes toward right, as* STAFF *comes*
on wheeling trolley with a large metal jug and some wash
bowls.)
Good morning to you, Staff.

STAFF : Morning.
(ASH *goes off.* STAFF *glances at Bed 5, then turns to Bed 4.*)
Doctor! Wakey-wakey . . . rise and shine.
(REES *raises his head, looks at her sternly. She moves on*
towards the left.)

FOSTER : Hullo, Staff.

STAFF : How's Mister Foster? Full of the joys of Spring?

FOSTER : Bearing up . . .

STAFF : That's the way . . . come on, Kenneth, stir your stumps.
Don't be late your last morning. . . .
(*Goes off left.* FOSTER *and* REES *watch. Offstage* KEN *begins*
coughing.)

FOSTER : Coughing well this morning, Kenneth.
(*Coughing continues and* KEN *comes on, carrying his*
towel, wearing a hospital dressing-gown. He is lighting a
cigarette as he crosses. He throws down the match and

11

goes off right.)

Don't throw the match down, son. Someone's got to pick it up.

REES: He smokes too much, that boy.

FOSTER: Morning, Doctor.

REES: Killed this fellow too, the cough.

FOSTER: Mister Lucas?

REES: Smoked too much.

FOSTER: With a chest like his, yes.

REES: Sixty-five, you know, that's all he was. I'm eighty-two, but I could have knocked spots off him.

FOSTER: I hope I'll be as fit as you at eighty-two.

REES: No, he's dead. He died last night.

FOSTER (*louder*): I say if I'm as fit as you at eighty, I shan't complain.

REES: Eighty-*two.*

FOSTER: Ah!

(REES *leans back.* MACKIE *wakes in Bed 6. He groans and* FOSTER *looks at him.*)

Cheer up, sir, you're still alive.

MACKIE: So I see. More's the pity.

REES: But Lucas has gone. That should please you.

MACKIE: A step in the right direction.

(REES *and* FOSTER *laugh.* REES *leans back again.* FOSTER *puts on his radio earphones.*)

SCENE TWO

Light grown warmer.

SWEET, *a plump English nurse wearing glasses, comes from the right bringing a screen on wheels. This she stands around Bed 3. She goes off and returns with another screen and closes in Bed 3 completely.*

12

LOACH *has come from the right. He wears a dark grey, slept-in suit and carries a raincoat on his arm. He looks lost.*

SWEET *comes forward to meet him with pyjamas and a hospital dressing-gown.*

SWEET: Good morning. You've no pyjamas?

LOACH: No.

(She leads him to the bed.)

SWEET: Change into these. I'll come for your clothes in a minute.

(She guides him through the screens. ASH *comes on, left, with an unfinished basket.* FOSTER *takes off earphones.* SWEET *comes to him.* ASH *finds an armchair.)*

How's my basket coming on, Mister Ash?

ASH: Not so dusty, nurse.

SWEET: You're slow.

ASH: Slow but sure.

*(*LAKE, *another West Indian nurse, comes from the right wheeling a dirty-linen receptacle. She checks a list.)*

LAKE: Which bed are we stripping?

SWEET *(coming down)*: Kenneth's. He's going out this morning.

LAKE: Which is Kenneth?

SWEET: Surely you know Kenny?

LAKE *(half-aside to* AUDIENCE*)*: They all look the same to me.

SWEET: The old ones, I daresay, but he's only nineteen.

LAKE *(checking list)*: Multiple fractures?

SWEET: Yes.

LAKE: I remember.

SWEET: Of course, you're married. Even so I should have thought you'd remember Kenny——

(They go off, left.)

FOSTER: Doing a spot of work on your basket?

ASH: I hope I never see another basket, to be quite frank.

(An OLD WOMAN *in a flowered dress and white hat comes from right and goes to* MACKIE'*s bed.)*

OLD WOMAN: Good morning. I have a message for you. It's that God gave His only begotten Son that whosoever

13

believeth in Him should not perish but have everlasting life.

MACKIE: He's welcome to it.

OLD WOMAN: Isn't it wonderful news? The best ever. There is no death.

MACKIE: I'm dying.

OLD WOMAN: Dying only to live.

MACKIE: Oh, all right.

OLD WOMAN: God bless you and get well soon.

(*She gives him a card. He drops it unread. She goes to Bed 5.*)

Good day. I have a message for you. It's that God gave His only begotten Son to save us. Us—that's you and me and everyone. So you need only believe and you'll have everlasting life. God bless you and get well soon.

(*No reaction from the patient. She puts a card between his fingers and turns to* REES, *who is asleep.*)

Good morning.

(*He wakes and turns his head to her.*)

I've brought you a message. Good news.

REES: From my wife, is it?

OLD WOMAN: God gave His only begotten Son to save us.

REES: I thought it was about the taxi.

OLD WOMAN: All of us—you, me——

REES: Is there any message about the taxi?

OLD WOMAN: Every one of us.

REES: You could get them to hurry it up.

(*He grasps her hand but she gently disengages herself and steps back.*)

OLD WOMAN: Bless you and get well soon.

(*She gives him a text and he stares at it. She goes to Bed 2.* FOSTER *has the phones on.*)

Good morning.

FOSTER (*takes off phones*): How d'you do?

OLD WOMAN: Have you heard the news?

FOSTER: I was just about to.

14

OLD WOMAN: God so loved the world that he gave His only begotten Son that whosoever believeth in Him should not perish but have everlasting life.

FOSTER: Right-i-o.

OLD WOMAN: The best news ever. There is no death.

FOSTER: I've got the greatest possible respect for other people's beliefs but if what you say is true——

OLD WOMAN: God bless you and get well soon.

FOSTER: ——where does that put Mr. Lucas? He was in the next bed here——

(*She gives him a card and goes off left.* LOACH *comes from screens, now wearing gown and pyjamas, carrying his clothes. He looks about uncertainly.*)

REES: I don't want to bother you. (*Holds out hand towards* LOACH, *who goes closer.*) Yes, I thought as much. You've brought my clothes. (*Grasps* LOACH's *clothes with both hands.*)

LOACH: Hang on——

REES: Only my wife's expecting me home to tea and I can't walk the streets in pyjamas.

LOACH: They're mine.

REES: There's a taxi waiting below but all my togs are in Sister's room, so——

(*They are struggling with the clothes as* SWEET *comes on, left.*)

——if you're passing, perhaps on the way back, you'd be so kind as too——

SWEET: Not being naughty again, are we, doctor?

REES: This gentleman's kindly offered to fetch my clothes.

SWEET: What about some bye-byes?

REES: Earlier on a lady brought me a message from my wife about the taxi . . . but my eyes are going . . . perhaps you——

(*Shows her the text, which she glances at.*)

SWEET: Now shall we tuck in nice and cosy——

REES: Only the meter will be ticking away down there . . .

15

SWEET: —and get some sleepy-byes?

REES: Some what?

SWEET: D'you want a bottle?

REES: I want my clothes.

SWEET: Let's see, shall we?

(*Tries to put hand under bedclothes but* REES *slaps it away*)

REES: Take your bloody hands off me.

SWEET: I don't call that very nice behaviour.

REES: Been eating boiled sweets again, I can smell them on your breath.

SWEET: More personal remarks?

REES: Never get your weight down that way.

SWEET: I've told you before——

REES: Try Banting's diet. (*to* FOSTER.) Banting was so fat he had to go downstairs backwards. (*Laughs at this and wipes eyes with sheet.*

SWEET: That must have been before the Ark. Everything's changed since you were in practice all those years ago. Don't forget that. You're the patient here, not the doctor. (*She has reached under the clothes and now brings out a bottle full of urine.*)

Telling fibs too! Now lie down like a good boy and nurse will fetch you another. And I'll take those . . . thank you.

(SWEET *takes* LOACH's *clothes and goes off.* REES *leans back on the pillow, exhausted.* LOACH *sidles away towards the stove.* ASH *is still at his basket.* LOACH *warms his hands.* LAKE *has come on and takes off one of the screens.*)

LOACH: Nice to see a fire.

ASH: It's not alight.

LOACH: Marvellous, isn't it?

ASH: Spot of bother with Dr. Rees?

LOACH: He Welsh or something?

ASH: Welsh, yes.

LOACH: I could tell the brogue.

ASH: Eighty-two. Stroke. Left him paralysed on one side.

16

Also his brain seems at times as sound as a bell, another
time completely in the grip of some delusion about a
taxi. He must know he's never going out of here alive,
but he won't give in. Spunky old blighter.

(SWEET *returns with a clean bottle.*)

SWEET: All right now?

(REES *nods, takes the bottle, puts it under.*)

That's nurse's favourite boy.

(*She goes, taking* LOACH's *other screen.*)

ASH: In the corner, Mister Flagg: bladder trouble and
complications. He was in theatre yesterday. I find, if they
keep you in the end beds, you can prepare to meet
your Maker.

LOACH: That end?

ASH: Where they can reach you easily.

LOACH: I'm only third from the end.

ASH: We all start *off* near the end. Under observation. But
we slowly work our way along to the furthest window
by the balcony.

LOACH: Long as we know.

ASH: That bed just happened to fall vacant this morning.

(SWEET *crosses from right to left.*)

Next to you on the other side Desmond Foster, coronary.
Young for that, only forty. Then me, Mervyn Ash,
tummy ulcer.

(*Offers his hand.* LOACH *shakes it.*)

Been here a fortnight so far. On a blotting paper diet.
Tapioca, semolina, boiled fish, chicken. The merest
glimpse of semolina makes me heave. Always has. Don't
ask me why.

(LOACH *is paying no attention. He looks frightened.* ASH
observes him closely. LOACH *pulls himself together.*)

LOACH: Who's the old boy by the door?

ASH: Mister Mackie. They've pulled him through once or
twice but he's lost the will.

(TYLER *comes on right in wheelchair.*)

17

TYLER: Hullo, Doc. How's Doc this morning?
    (REES *looks up.*)
    Lovely morning, Des. . . .
FOSTER: Been out?
TYLER: Over to physio. Lovely Spring day.
    (REES *waves his hand.*)
    Keep smiling, Mervyn.
ASH: We do our best, friend.
    (TYLER *goes off.*)
REES: How d'you do?
ASH: Gone now, doctor. He's gone. (*Then to* LOACH). Friend
    Tyler from up the ward. Had both legs off at the knee.
    Some malignant growth, I'm not too sure. But what a
    wonderful spirit! Always full of beans. How enviable!
    Me, I'm up and down like a yo-yo. And when I'm down
    —by George! Which accounts for the ulcer, I suppose.
    And this endless therapy. Electric therapy, physiotherapy,
    occupational therapy. Chit-chat with the trick cyclist.
    Marquetry and basket making. Which, quite frankly, has
    the same appeal to me as semolina.
    (*Laughs and gives* LOACH *a playful nudge.* LAKE *comes
    from left, wheeling linen-basket.*)
LAKE: New patient ready for a bath?
ASH: That's you.
LOACH: What?
LAKE: Get a towel from your locker, have a bath.
    (*She goes off, right.* LOACH *goes to his bed.*)
FOSTER: They keep you busy here. They'll wake you up to
    give you a sleeping tablet.
LOACH: Yeah? She better watch it. No blackie pushes me
    around.
    (KEN *comes in from left, now wearing black motor-cycle
    gear. Across the back is some fiendish emblem. He carries
    his helmet and a grip with his belongings.*)
KEN: I'm off then. Ta-ta, mate.
ASH: Goodbye, Kenny. Take care on that motor-bike now.

18

My father used to say "Better five minutes late in this world than fifty years early in the next!"

KEN: He sounds like a lot of fun.

ASH: He was wonderful. I only mean, if you can't consider the pedestrians, at least think about your own skin.

KEN (shrugs): People don't stop screwing for fear of knob-rot. (goes to MACKIE.) Cheero, Dad. Get well soon.

ASH: I'm afraid you've got a one-track mind.

KEN (leaving MACKIE): I ain't got a one-track mind.

ASH: Sounds like it.

KEN: Who wouldn't have a one-track mind in here?

FOSTER: Should learn to control your appetite.

KEN: I touched up that fat nurse behind the screens couple of times but she wouldn't cock her leg. (Goes to FLAGG.) Tarrah, Dad, you'll soon be out of here. (Comes a few steps from him.) He ain't got long to go.

FOSTER: You're old enough to have learnt respect.

KEN (to REES): Bye-bye, Doc. Get well soon, me old mate.

REES (stirring): You the driver?

KEN: Eh?

REES: My wife waiting down below in the taxi?

KEN: No, I'm Ken. Just off home.

REES: You a patient is it?

(SWEET has wandered on from left.)

KEN: Yes. Cheerio. Get well soon. (Comes away.) He's bleeding ga-ga.

SWEET: You're never walking through the streets like that?

KEN: My girl's brought the bike.

SWEET: Oh, really? Must be school holidays then.

KEN: No, she ought to be in school but she took the morning off to get me. I'll be taking her straight home. See my animals have been looked after, then get round to her. Tarrah, mate.

FOSTER: Bye and keep out of trouble. You're old enough to have consideration for other people. I've been out some-times in my minibus, suddenly there's several of you

19

jokers in formation coming towards me on my side of
the road.

(KEN *starts laughing*.)

I've got the kids in the back more often than not and I
daren't swerve for fear of hurting them. Can't pull up,
there's a car behind.

KEN: That's quite a giggle but I've never gone into no one
doing that. My last pile-up I was dodging a dog. I've
never killed an animal. Never would. I'm animal-minded.

ASH: Hitler iiked animals.

KEN: Who?

ASH: Hitler. *He* was opposed to blood sports.

KEN: Who's he when he's at home?

ASH: Never heard of Hitler?

FOSTER: German dictator during the last war. He——

KEN: Oh, yeah, Belsen and that. I read about it. Must have
been a giggle in there.

ASH: A what?

KEN: All them naked women. I read about it.

SWEET: Goodbye, Kenneth. I expect we shall see you here
again.

KEN: Not if I can help it.

SWEET: Twice so far.

KEN: No more.

SWEET: We'll keep your bed warm. If you've no objection.

KEN: All depends how.

(*He approaches her. She retreats but he catches her by
Bed 3.*)

SWEET: Now then——

(*Pushes her back on to it and lies on top of her.*)

—that's enough . . . stop it!

(KEN *is laughing*.)

FOSTER: You'll get into trouble.

ASH: You've no respect at all.

KEN: Hear that? Get you into trouble?

SWEET: Leave me alone.

ASH: That was Mr. Lucas's bed.

LOACH: It's *my* bed. I ain't even laid in it yet.

(KEN *releases* SWEET.)

KEN: You got my address? It's on my card. Pop round some time, have a cup of tea. Only my gran in during the day and she's stone deaf. (*He addresses the ward in general.*) Bye-bye, all! Get well soon!

(*Goes down front stairs as a feeble reply is given.* SWEET *adjusts her uniform and smoothes* LOACH's *bed.*)

FOSTER: You all right, nurse?

SWEET: Thank you.

ASH: That's good riddance to bad rubbish.

REES (*waving his hand*): Goodbye to you!

ASH: He's gone long ago, Doctor.

LOACH: My bed, that is, haven't even laid in it.

SWEET: Aren't you meant to be in the bath?

LOACH: Eh?

SWEET: You're supposed to be in the bath.

LOACH: I'm getting a towel, me old mate.

SWEET: Hurry up then.

(*She goes off.*)

LOACH: Nobody tells me what to do. Which way's the bath?

(FOSTER *points.* LOACH *goes off right.* ASH *works on his basket.* FOSTER *stretches his arms.* MACKIE *groans with pain. Pause.*)

FOSTER: What's his trouble? The new man?

ASH: He didn't say. Looks a bit poverty stricken. No pyjamas or slippers of his own. His clothes very seedy. I used to tell my boys, a decent voice and a tailor-made suit will always put you a cut above the scum.

(OLD WOMAN *comes back from left.*)

OLD WOMAN: Good morning, have you heard the news?

ASH: Jesus died to give us life.

OLD WOMAN: There is no death.

ASH: I know.

OLD WOMAN: It's wonderful news.

ASH: It certainly is.

(*She gives him a text.*)

OLD WOMAN: God bless you.

ASH: Amen.

(*She goes off, down the front stairs.*)

FOSTER: They ought to stop her coming round.

ASH: I don't know.

FOSTER: People don't want religion when they're not feeling up to the mark. Very nice in its proper place but you don't want it rammed down your throat, do you?

ASH: I *am* religious, as a matter of fact.

FOSTER: I've got a great respect for other people's beliefs as long as it goes no further.

ASH: I believe in reincarnation.

FOSTER: There you are then.

(FOSTER *puts on the earphones to avoid further conversation.* ASH *would go on but sees there is no point.*)

SCENE THREE

BARNET *enters, pushing a wheelchair in a wide arc across the ward, arriving downstage facing the audience. As he goes, he is talking to the patients.*

BARNET: Come along, ladies, come along. Knickers on and stand by your beds. Those that can't stand, lie to attention.

(*Feeble laughs and cheers from the patients. Though* BARNET's *patter is addressed to the audience, the patients react.*)

SWEET *comes from right with a china feeder and gives* FLAGG *a drink of water.*)

22

No, it's wicked to laugh. I said to this old man in the next ward, I said, "Dad, you better watch your step," he said, "Why?" I said, "They're bringing in a case of syphilis." He said, "Well, it'll make a change from Lucozade."

(*Laughter and applause from patients.*)

SWEET: I didn't hear that remark.

BARNET: Whoops, sorry, nurse, I never saw you come on.

(*He ogles the audience and goes upstage with the chair.*)

SWEET: Is that a lovely drink, Mister Flagg?

BARNET: Come on, doctor, hands off, give it a rest, you'll be going blind. (*He winks at* FOSTER.)

REES: Shocking sight. A man being fed like a baby, through a spout. I can drink my tea and eat my dinner.

BARNET: Course you can.

REES: Mister Barnet, be a good fellow——

BARNET: What?

REES: —tell them to get a move on with my shoes and socks, where can I go without them?

BARNET: They've got to wait though.

REES: What for?

BARNET: Till your wife's been in.

REES: She *has* been in.

BARNET: No.

REES: Hasn't she?

BARNET: We haven't long had dinner, have we?

REES: Haven't we?

(*Pause.* REES *thinks.*)

BARNET: What d'you say to a spot of air, then? On the verandah. She might be in by then.

SWEET: There's a clever boy.

(*Puts feeder on locker as* FLAGG *lies back.*)

BARNET: And when she comes, no funny business!

REES (*smiling*): What d'you mean?

BARNET: Pulling her into bed.

(REES *laughs.* FOSTER *too.*)

23

No, well, it's not very nice. Front of all the visitors.

SWEET (*coming to help*): Don't make him laugh too much, he hasn't got a bottle.

REES: I don't want a bottle, I'm not a baby.

BARNET: You're a dirty old man.

(SWEET *throws back covers.*)

SWEET: Roly-poly on your bot-bot.

(*They swing his legs to the floor and lift him.*)

BARNET: Shall we dance?

SWEET: Ups-a-daisy!

BARNET: Shan't we put him in the chair?

SWEET: He needs exercise.

(*They begin to walk him, his arms around their necks, supporting his weight as he tries to find the use of his legs.*)

BARNET: Might make him a touch less lively when his wife comes in.

SWEET: There's a clever boy.

FOSTER: Go it, Doctor!

(*Cheers from patients.*)

BARNET: Which is why they invented rugby. Keep their minds off it.

SWEET: Off what?

(*Laughs.* REES *manages a few steps, then they drag him a few. He is laughing.*)

BARNET: What we got to keep your mind off, Doctor?

REES: I used to be a scrum-half. I could run like a rabbit.

BARNET: Not only run.

(*Whispers in* REES'S *ear.* REES *laughs, stops them walking.* BARNET *grins.*)

SWEET: Look-out, he's doing it!

(*She points at* REES'S *trousers.*)

BARNET: Jesus God!

SWEET: I'll get the chair, you hold him.

(*Goes for it. They are furthest from the bed.*)

BARNET: Why didn't you have a bottle when she asked you?

(REES *makes frightened sounds, begins to struggle.*)

Don't be a soppy old madam now. You'll fall.

24

(*But the struggle grows more desperate.* ASH *comes to help.*)

ASH: Now, Doctor——

  (REES *swings his arm and catches* ASH *across the head.*
  ASH *falls to the ground with a cry.* SWEET *brings the chair
  and* BARNET *drops* REES *into it.*)

SWEET: Naughty boy! Are you all right?

ASH: He caught me across the ear.

SWEET (*helping him up*): Have a rest.

BARNET: I'll get her a fresh pair of knickers.

  (*Goes off, right.* ASH *goes to an armchair.* SWEET *wheels*
  REES *back to his bed.*)

SWEET: Whatever am I going to do with this great big naughty
  boy?

FOSTER: You all right, Mister Ash?

ASH: Yes, yes. Took my breath away for a second.

MACKIE: Why are you keeping him alive? Like a baby?

SWEET (*packing* REES *into bed*): Now, now——

MACKIE: You know he'll never walk again——

SWEET: Mister Mackie, save it for a more suitable occasion.

MACKIE: We know, his wife knows——

  (BARNET *returns, gives pyjamas to* REES. FOSTER *begins
  singing Gaumont-British theme.*)

  But no, you keep the farce going——

  (*He gives up, coughing.*)

SWEET: Tuck up nice and warm and think of something nice.

BARNET (*to* AUDIENCE): Why don't you *all* think of something
  nice?

  (SWEET *finally goes off right.*)

SCENE FOUR

Lights dim upstage.
*Music begins and patients look up expectantly from their
positions. All those who are well enough watch the ensuing scene.*

Bright lights on a downstage area as a divan and screen rise into view. CLEO NORTON *lies on the divan wearing a shortie nightdress.* BARNET *has crossed down left and reads aloud from a paperback novel.*

BARNET: Her bedside alarm gave raucous tongue and Staff Nurse Cleo Norton awoke mid-afternoon suddenly, bewilderingly, and some moments passed before she could realise she was in her room at the nurses' residential hostel.
(STAFF *wakes in the bed and mimes to the narrative.*)
Her tousled hair and the rumpled sheets were evidence enough of a fitful sleep. If evidence she needed! She flounced over in bed, flung back the sheets petulantly and swung her lithe coffee-coloured legs round till her feet touched the pretty coconut mat she brought from Jamaica all those years ago.
Stretching langorously, she reached for her housecoat and wrapped it demurely around her trim figure.
(*She goes to a window and draws back curtains.*)
Outside, the same breeze was still sending newly-laundered white clouds scudding across the blue, like members of a *corps de ballet* obeying the behest of some unseen choreographer. Suddenly nauseated, she flung herself on the bed.

STAFF: What's the matter with you anyway, Cleo Norton?
BARNET: —she demanded of herself, half angrily. But the mad ecstatic leap of her heart had already told her.
STAFF: Neil!
BARNET: In the submarine strangeness of the night ward, young Doctor Neil Boyd's fingers had fleetingly touched hers. And his usually stern features had crumpled into a yearning smile. Their eyes had met and ricochetted away.
STAFF: This won't do.
BARNET: —She chastised herself ruefully.

(*Roughly she makes the bed, etc.*)

STAFF: Here you are, a woman of twenty-six, behaving like some love-sick teenager with a television idol.

BARNET: —she opined diagnostically.

STAFF: And yet——

BARNET: And yet——

(STAFF *shrugs and goes off behind the screen. Music swells.*)
In the ward, TYLER *comes from left to right in his chair.*)

TYLER: Charwallah ready?

ASH: Sssh!

(TYLER *goes off right.*
SWEET *and* LAKE *come up the front steps wearing outdoor cloaks over their uniforms.*)

SWEET: I keep saying ruefully to myself: this climb should get my weight down, but it doesn't! Ssssh! Cleo may be still in the Land of Nod. No, she's up. Sit down, Beth.
(LAKE *sits on bed.*)
I'll put on a kettle when she comes in. I feel so honoured you finally managed to come to tea. You're certainly hard to get, Beth Lake——

LAKE: Being a nurse and a married woman isn't any rest cure, believe me, Joyce Sweet.

SWEET: Just give me the chance.

LAKE: Don't be in a hurry, Joyce. You're young yet.

BARNET: Beth flashed her large, gleaming widely-spaced teeth.

SWEET: Guess I'm just the marrying kind, Beth. Listen, Beth.

LAKE: What is it, Joyce?

SWEET: Your husband drives a bus full of white passengers and you look after a ward full of white patients— Don't you ever get hopping mad, Beth?

LAKE: Mad? No, Joyce. Why?

SWEET: When you think of the way some white people treat coloured people, I wonder you're not tempted to turn off their saline solutions or something . . .

LAKE: Oh, no, those people shouldn't be hated. They should be pitied. And understood.

27

SWEET: And when you think that the Health Service would pack up tomorrow if you all went back where you came from. Crikey! I'm surprised you bother to stay, Beth, honestly!

(STAFF *comes in, now wearing her uniform, or some of it.*)

BARNET: Cleo Norton breezed back into the room, her pert figure now trimly encased in the crisp uniform. She grinned a sunny welcome.

STAFF: Hullo, Joyce, hullo, Beth.

BOTH: Hullo, Cleo.

STAFF: How was duty?

SWEET: Methinks you don't have to be mad to work here but it helps.

STAFF: Why, what on earth happened?

LAKE: A couple of appendicectomies, no progress for the spontaneous pneumothorax . . .

SWEET: Matron decided to come inspecting just as the Registrar was doing a lumbar puncture . . .

STAFF (*laughing*): Situation normal.

SWEET: And the inguinal hernia needed morphine and Sister said I could do it——

LAKE: Oh, yes, and I didn't tell you, when I went to her room soon after we'd admitted the diabetic, I found Sister with young Doctor Boyd and they were holding hands.

BARNET: Cleo Norton flushed and her hand flew to her mouth.

(STAFF *steps back, her hand flying to her face.*)

SWEET: Ooops!

LAKE: What on earth's the matter? What have I said?

BARNET: Cleo stared speechless at Beth Lake, S.R.N., and then —wordlessly—fled the room.

(STAFF *bursts into tears and goes off.*)

SWEET: That's torn it!

LAKE: But—what on earth——?

BARNET: —queried Beth Lake, crinkling her endearing button of a nose.

SWEET: Not your fault, Beth. You weren't to know Cleo's sweet on young Doctor Boyd.

BARNET: It was Nurse Lake's turn to flush.

LAKE: Mrs. Clever Boots——

BARNET: —She murmured at last——

LAKE: Mrs. Open-your-mouth-and-put-your-big-foot-in-it.

SWEET: Never mind. You could have been wrong in what you saw.

LAKE: They *were* holding hands.

SWEET: Was there a sheepish grin on his lean, craggy features?

LAKE (*thinks, shakes her head*): A puzzled frown.

SWEET: Then there's hope yet.

LAKE: But listen, Joyce, isn't old Mr. Boyd, the young doctor's bluff father, bitterly opposed to mixed marriages?

SWEET: Crikey, yes! He's a terrible diehard.

LAKE: But what a surgeon!

SWEET: And just a tick, Beth! Doesn't Sister McPhee hail from North of the Border?

LAKE: And wait a minute, Joyce, isn't Dr. Neil unusually respectful to his father?

SWEET: And hang on, Beth, isn't Mr. Boyd an eligible widower?

LAKE: I wonder——

SWEET: You mean——?

BARNET: They stared at each other wordlessly.

(*Music swells as front lights fade on this.*
LAKE and SWEET step out of the room and go up into the
ward. SWEET goes off left and LAKE goes to MACKIE's bed.)

SCENE FIVE

Warm light.

LOACH *comes from right. The patients all have thermometers in their mouths.* LAKE *gets* MACKIE's *chart.*

29

LAKE: Have you had your bowels open?

MACKIE: My dear woman——

ASH: You've been a long time with the doctors, friend.

(LOACH *turns to him suspiciously but says nothing*.)

I hope they've got you sorted out now.

LOACH: Suppose you haven't got such a thing as a cigarette?

(ASH *looks at his watch*.)

ASH: You're in luck, it's smoking time from two to five.

(LAKE *takes* MACKIE's *pulse and reads his temperature. She writes the result on his chart and afterwards goes to* FLAGG.)

LOACH: Ta. Half these doctors, they turn round and tell you not to smoke but half of them smoke more than what you or I do. Ta.

ASH: I hope they gave you some dinner.

LOACH: Yes. (*He smokes with a cupped hand, as though hiding the cigarette from view. He now edges towards the stove.*)

ASH: I had my usual boiled fish and semolina. Which frankly has about as much appeal to me as basket-making.

LOACH: What d'you mean by that? Basket-making?

ASH: Occupational therapy. I take it with a pinch of salt. However, it's helped to pass the time. I was horribly depressed when I came in here. Largely because I abhor my work. Clerical. I'm a clerk, if you please. Mechanical, futile, dreary to the nth degree. I say to my fellow-inmates in our prison-without-bars: this is mechanical drudgery. And when they tell me it's a living, I come back quick as a flash: man shall not live by bread alone.

(LAKE *notes* FLAGG's *temperature and goes to* REES.)

I see in the daily rag now where they've got a computer thingummyjig can perform a clerk's entire lifework in ten minutes. Highly gratifying. I've known better things, there's the jolly old rub.

Handling the young is my vocation. My first year at teachers' college was a benediction. I felt: I have come home, this is where I belong. Amongst people of my own kidney.

LAKE: Have you had your bowels open?

REES: What?

LAKE: Have you had your bowels open?

REES: Yes.

ASH: I've always been able to handle boys. Why did I leave it? You may well ask. A matter of preferment. Nepotism. Muggins here didn't give the secret handshake, never got tiddly in the right golf-club. I didn't have the bishop's ear. You scratch my back, I'll scratch yours. I wasn't smarmey enough by half.

(LAKE *brings* LOACH's *thermometer.*)

LAKE (*to* LOACH): Under your tongue. And that patient, not so much talking, while I take your temperature.

ASH: Hunkey dorey, nurse.

(*Puts thermometer in mouth.* LAKE *goes to* REES, *reads his temperature and notes it on his chart. Then she goes to* FOSTER.

ASH *moves to his locker and rummages.* LOACH *takes out thermometer and drags on his cigarette.*)

FOSTER (*reading*): Ninety-eight point two, nurse.

(LAKE *takes it from him, reads it and notes on his chart.* SWEET *removes* FLAGG's *drip, takes it off right.*)

LAKE: Ninety-eight point two.

(ASH *returns with books and a photograph.*)

ASH: I never lost my interest in boys. Not even through ten years of pen-pushing. That's Gordon. (*Shows* LOACH *the photograph.*)

LAKE: Have you had your bowels open?

FOSTER: Twice.

ASH: He's my own boy.

LOACH: Got no clothes on, has he? Not by the look of it.

ASH: Swimming trunks.

LOACH: Flesh coloured.

ASH: That was taken at this private boarding school I put him

31

to. Super duper place in its own grounds, down in Kent.
(SWEET *comes back. Tidying, moving to the stove.*)
You've met my boy, nurse?

SWEET: Very nicely spoken boy.

ASH: They take trouble with elocution. Good speech is half the
battle, *carte blanche* to the inner circle.

LOACH: Inner circle?

ASH: Where the good jobs are, where decisions are made.
Once you can break into that, you never look back. My
trouble was I never broke into the inner circle. (*looks
at photo.*) He doesn't live with me any more. Old enough
to take care of himself. I'm expecting him in for a visit
one of these days but it's a long way to come. . . . I accept
that. . . . If you're interested in reading matter, these might
while away an hour or two. School magazines.

LOACH: Not much of a reader, know what I mean?'

ASH: Time drags, in here.

LOACH: They can't keep you in here. If you don't want to
stay. I shall turn round and tell them, if they start that
with me.

SWEET: Better now?

ASH: Easy, friend, hold you horses. Nobody said they can.

LOACH: Once they've found out . . .

ASH: They'll fix you up, don't worry.

LOACH: Once they find out who I am. Once they can tell me
that, I'll be out of here like a . . . what d'you call it . . . ?

ASH: Who you are?

LOACH: Once the police get on to that.

ASH: Who you *are*?

LOACH: Not that I want the police sticking their noses into
my business. I didn't *ask* them, know what I mean?
(SWEET *eases* MACKIE.)

MACKIE: Oh, hell! This is hell.

LOACH: But soon as they put me straight on that, I'm off.
They try to get me to take the cure, they got another
think coming . . .

LAKE (*coming to them*): Too much talking, this patient.

ASH: Naughty boy, hold out your hand.

LAKE: Put that in your mouth.

(LOACH *throws his dog-end into the stove and puts the thermometer in his mouth.* LAKE *gets* ASH's *chart.*)

ASH: Nurse, are you going to move me along into Kenneth's place? One nearer the balcony?

SWEET: Time you had a rest, new patient.

LAKE (*to* ASH): Do you *want* to move along?

LOACH: Where's that, me old mate?

SWEET: Into bed, come on.

ASH (*to* LAKE): I'm on the mend, I deserve a move. One nearer the balcony is one nearer the outside world. Not that the outside world is anything to write home about.

SWEET: Still talking, Mister Ash?

ASH: *My* outside world, at any rate.

SWEET: Sit by your bed, stop talking and give the thermometer a chance.

(LOACH *has gone to his bed.* ASH *now goes to his.* SWEET *tidies the armchairs.*)

ASH: No peace for the wicked.

SWEET: Stop talking, I said.

LAKE: Have your bowels been opened?

(ASH *holds up one finger. She writes it on his chart.* ASH *sits by his bed,* LOACH *gets into his.*

LAKE *writes down* ASH's *and* LOACH's *temperatures. In due course, the nurses go off left.*)

SCENE SIX

Music.

BOYD *comes on as the lights come up downstage. He is smoking or cleaning a pipe. Perhaps wearing a pullover.* NEIL *comes to him, wearing a suit.*

NEIL: You wanted to see me, father?

BOYD: Och, there you are, Neil. Come in, come in.
(BOYD's *Scots accent is heavier in this scene.*)

NEIL: If it's about the informality of my ward-rounds, you
can save you breath to cool your porridge. I believe I
am the patients' servant, not the other way round. I'm
not going to have a lot of ceremony——

BOYD: Now, now, dinna fash yesel. It's noo that. We agree
to differ on the question of how to treat our fellows.

NEIL: Aye. You, the firm believer, seem to regard the weak
and infirm as inferiors. I, the sceptic, behave to them as
to my equals.

BOYD: Happily, the Almighty, in His infinite wisdom, has not
denied us the use of our common sense. We have as our
practice the world as it is, not as it might be. Which has
a bearing on the matter in hand. Urmph! In Paradise, it
would not be frowned on for white folk and black to
mingle.

NEIL: Now just a tick——

BOYD: However, as you know, we are not in Paradise. We are
in North London. You are a house physician in a large
teaching hospital and Nurse Norton is a junior member
of the staff. The poor wee girl can only be hurt by all this.
Sister MacPhee can only be hurt by it.

NEIL: Sister MacPhee——?

BOYD: I know ye'll come back to her in the end——

NEIL: Come back to her——?

BOYD: But you're noo in any position to play fast and loose——

NEIL: Fast and loose?

BOYD: And wee Mary MacPhee used to take you to school
with your wee satchel on your shoulder——

NEIL: Satchel on my shoulder?

BOYD: She was your chielhood sweetheart.
(*Pause.*)

NEIL: Aye, father, she was my chielhood sweetheart. But
I'm no a chiel the noo. I'm a man. I've told Mary how

I feel about Cleo—I want to marry her——

BOYD: Urmph? You trying to prove something, son?

NEIL: Prove something?

BOYD: A gesture, is it?

NEIL: Gesture?

BOYD: You can't hurt me. I'm here to fight. But you can hurt your mother.

NEIL: Mother's dead.

BOYD: Aye, she's dead. And almost her last wish was that you two should marry, that Mary should be one of the family. And now ye say ye're taking a wee coloured girl to wife and . . . Mary is to be left on the shelf. At thirty. Have you thought of that, son? While you're so busy with your noble sentiments? Have you given a wee thought to puir bonnie Mary at the age of thirty? Have ye? (*Music.*)

SCENE SEVEN

The opening blue light.
All the patients sleeping or trying to.
A steady groundbass of snores.
After a while, ASH stirs.

ASH: That boy—I warn you . . .
    (*Incoherent speech follows.*)
    (*Silence again.*)
    After some time, one of the sleepers farts very violently, then groans with relief.)
    (*Silence.*)
    (*After another pause, REES sits up.*)

REES (*shouts*): I haven't got a change of clothing here!
    (*Resentful groans.*)

35

Not even a clean pair of socks. They can't expect the
taxi man to wait there till the cows come home . . . could
at least send him a cup of tea.

FOSTER: Give us a rest, Doc.

ASH: There's a good chap.

REES: Who pays for the bloody tea, I'd like to know?
(FOSTER *laughs*.)

FOSTER: He's on about tea.

REES: Take him a cup, you damned old Scrooge. It's like
gnat's piss anyway.

FOSTER: No taxi drivers this time of night.
(STAFF *comes on from right.*)

STAFF: Doctor, you've let me down again.

REES: You let me have my clothes, I'll show you the taxi.

STAFF (*settling him*): I'll make you a nice hot drink, will you
promise faithfully to let us get a bit of shut-eye?

REES: Poisoned drinks! No, thank you very much. Nor your
sleeping drugs and formaldehydes and paraldehydes——

FOSTER (*laughing*): Knows all about it.

REES: Trying to kill me off.

MACKIE: No such luck.

STAFF: Now be a good boy.

MACKIE: They're compelled by law to keep us going.

STAFF: Not tonight, Mister Mackie.

REES (*struggling*): What I want is sound legal advice! I want to
know what my chances are if it comes to litigation!

TYLER (*off left*): Nurse, look here, quick!
(*Sounds of coughing and choking.*)

STAFF: Now, lie down, while I tuck you in . . .

VOICE: Nurse——

STAFF: Coming!
(*She goes quickly off left.*)

REES: Is there a legal gentleman here?

MACKIE: There's no taxi, you crackpot. Die with dignity, for
Christ's sake.

FOSTER: Try to help the nurse while you're——

36

REES: Help! They're trying to kill me off.

FOSTER: No, listen, while we're in here, we must do as we're told——

REES: Never done that all my life——

FOSTER: I dare say, but even so——

REES: And I've had a good life.

FOSTER: Plenty more to come too.

TYLER (*off left*): Not if you don't belt up, there won't be.

FOSTER (*quietly*): Night, night, Doctor.

REES (*angrily*): Who was that?

FOSTER: Never mind.

> (*Both settle.*)
> (*Silence.*)
> (*At last the fart and the groan of relief are heard again.*)

MACKIE: Born in pig-sties, some of these people.

> (STAFF NURSE *crosses from left to right and off.*
> FLAGG, *Bed 5, climbs out and stands, leaning on the bed for support. He wears only a pyjama jacket and has a bandaged pelvis. He begins moving along, step by step.*)

REES: Get back, you, Mister——

> REES *throws back covers and stands.* FLAGG *is at the bed's end.* REES *takes a step towards him, cries out and falls. Lies there cursing.* FOSTER *climbs out and goes to* REES. *Various bed lights are going on.*)

FOSTER: Mister Ash!

> (ASH *wakes, sees, gets out.*)

ASH: Now, now, Mister Flagg, where d'you think you're off to? Half-past twelve, there's nowhere open.

> (*Tries to persuade* FLAGG *back to bed.* FOSTER *struggles with* REES.)

FOSTER: You all right, Doctor?

REES: How's the *old* fellow?

> (ASH *gets* FLAGG *back to bed, pulls up the bars to enclose him.*)

FOSTER: He's fine.

ASH (*turning to* REES): Whoops-a-daisy!

(*And they lift him into bed.*)

You shouldn't be doing this.

FOSTER: I'm all right.

REES: I was afraid he'd start to tear his bandage off . . . he ripped the skin he'd know all about it.

ASH: That's a good chap.

REES: If he'd opened the scar . . .

FOSTER: You all right now, Doc?

REES: (*to* ASH): You one of the nursing staff? No.

ASH: No. Ash. Tummy ulcer.

REES: Nothing to worry about. You'll soon be out. Unlike poor old Flagg there and—you, sir, what's your name?

FOSTER: Foster.

REES: Yes. They won't be with us long, I'm afraid.

ASH: Baloney, doctor, so much baloney. Back to bed, Desmond, I can manage.

(FOSTER *returns to bed.*)

REES: Flagg's had chronic urethritis. Makes your dicky sore. And this gentleman—where's he gone——?

ASH: Snuggle down, now, leave it to the Doctors.

REES: I *am* a Doctor.

ASH: I know, yes.

(REES *begins sobbing.*)

REES: See the way I fell down? I didn't think . . . went to walk and . . . in my youth I ran like a rabbit . . . I was Area High Jump Champion (*cries again*).

ASH: There, there . . .

(STAFF *returns, crossing quickly from right to left with a tray and hypodermic.*)

STAFF: All right?

ASH: Thank you, Staff . . .

REES: I beg your pardon. We're a highly emotional people. Ask anyone.

MACKIE: Sentimental and sloppy, if you ask me.

ASH: We *didn't* ask you, Mister Mackie.

REES: Much obliged to you.

ASH: Sleep well. (*Settles him and prepares to go.*)

REES: Could I trouble you? A bottle?

ASH: A bottle.

REES: I want to wee-wee.

ASH: I'll get you one.

(*Goes off right. Lights go out. Everyone settles.* STAFF *returns from left.* ASH, *returning, meets her.*)

STAFF: Where have you been, Mister Ash?

ASH: Getting this for the Doctor.

STAFF: Thank you. Go back to bed now.

(ASH *goes to his bed.* STAFF *goes to* REES *with the bottle.*)

FOSTER: This new fellow wasn't exactly helpful.

ASH: Heavy sleeper possibly.

FOSTER: His eyes were open, I saw them.

ASH: Oh, well . . .

FOSTER: He's awake now. He's laying there awake. Walking patient too. Didn't move a muscle. I hope he's listening to what I say.

STAFF: Sssh!

(*She puts the bottle into the Doctor's bed. She turns to check* FLAGG, *then comes round the Doctor's bed, tucking him in.*)

LOACH (*quietly*): Tell you what, me old mate——

STAFF: Are you talking to me?

LOACH: —I'm feeling a bit dry. And chilly. You could let me have a drink.

STAFF: All right. Which would you like——?

LOACH: Brandy——

STAFF: Ovaltine or Horlicks?

(REES *sits up, staring ahead.*)

LOACH: Can't seem to stomach it. Lays too heavy on the stomach sort of thing, you get my meaning? Drop of brandy.

(REES *sits back quickly.*)

STAFF: No. You go to sleep.

LOACH: I got the shakes a bit, see . . .

STAFF: Have a sleeping draught.

(*Pause. She bends over* REES *and examines him.*)

LOACH: Can't keep me in here——

STAFF: Sssh!

FOSTER: Belt up.

(*She leans further over* REES.)

(*Drums and music.*)

(*Downstage* BARNET *comes on in a travelling spot, pushing a trolley covered with a white cloth.*)

(*Front-cloth business with the spot, losing and finding it.*)

BARNET (*to* SPOTMAN): You'll get your cards tomorrow.

(*then to* AUDIENCE) No, but seriously. Sometimes the first call you get when you come on duty is: bring your trolley. I like to see my apparatus laid out like a tea-service, every instrument in its place. With a nice white cloth. It really brings me on to see that ... you know? (*Gooses himself.*) Here! (*Slaps his own hand.*) Lady there knows what I mean. No, but look—(*whips off cloth, shows articles as he names*): Wash bowl, sponges, nail brush and file. Safety razor, scissors, tweezers. Cotton-wool, carbolic soap. Shroud.

(*Covers it again.* STAFF *has gone off.*)

Covered with a sheet, 'case one of the other patients catching a butcher's thinks it's all for him. So anyway I get the call. Ward such-and-such, bed so-and-so. Screens already up, of course.

(NURSES *have been putting screens round* REES'S *bed.*)

First you strip the patient down, then you wash him spotless with carbolic. Cut the nails—they can scag the shroud. Shave the face and trim the head. Comb what's left. Well, relatives don't want to find themselves mourning a scruff. Now the cotton-wool. Can anyone tell me what I do with that? (*Reacts to same* WOMAN *in audience.*) You're right, madam, absolutely right. Been making that answer all your life and for the first time it's accurate, not just vulgar. Yes. We have to close the

40

apertures, the points that might evacuate bodily fluids. Miss one out, they'll raise Cain in the mortuary. Lug-holes, cake-holes, nose-holes, any other holes, all right madam thank you very much indeed! (*More ogling the* WOMAN.) What next? Tie the how's-your-father with a reef-knot. Seriously. You reckon I'm in jest? You'll all be getting it sooner or later. Yes, missis, even you, in a manner of speaking. (*Moves and looks at screens.*) Thank you very much, miss.

(*An* ORIENTAL NURSE *comes on, takes the trolley.* BARNET *pats her rump as she passes. She gives shocked magician's-assistant smile to* AUDIENCE, *goes off.* BARNET *has gone to other side to meet, rolling on, another vehicle, like a stretcher but with a hooped hood.*)

(*Sings.*) Roll along, covered wagon, roll along. No, listen! I must say this in all seriousness. Everything within reason is done to spare you the sight of an actual cadaver. This hooped cover, the screens.

(NURSES *cover the exit from* REES'*s bed with screens.*)

A screened passageway is put up all the way to the door, as with royalty going to the toilet. You've heard about that, haven't you? If the monarch is unusually tall, attentive observers can spot the coronet bobbing up and down all the way to the velvet convenience.

(*Pushes hooped trolley upstage.* NURSE *catches it and takes it behind screens.*)

No, I don't wish to give the wrong impression. I'm sure I speak for my colleagues throughout the business when I say that we show every conceivable respect the deceased is due. We may hate the sight of them when they're living but once they've passed on, they get the full going-over. And I don't know about you, but I find that thought consoling. Whatever kind of shit is thrown at us during our long and dusty travail, we can at least feel confident that, after our final innings, as we make our way to that great pavilion in the sky—no, come on— we

41

shall be a credit to Britain's barbers, the National Health and—last but by no means least—our mothers. Thank you very much indeed.

(*Exit to music.*)

(NURSES *have removed screens, leaving* REES's *space vacant, the bed gone.*)

(*Blackout.*)

SCENE EIGHT

Daylight. Everyone in bed.

TYLER (*offstage. Sings*): We'll find a perfect peace
Where joys will never cease
(*Crosses left to right in his chair.*)
And let the rest of the world go by.
(*A few* PATIENTS *cheer.* TYLER *goes off.*)

ASH: Keeps marvellously cheerful.

LOACH: Go on.
(SWEET *comes in from right with letters.*)

SWEET: Second post. One for you, Mr. Ash.

ASH: Thank you. My son Gordon, perhaps to say he's coming in to see me.

SWEET: And the last for Mr. Flagg. I don't know, nothing for me again. You'd think some nice young man would send me his love.

FOSTER: Will I do, nurse?

SWEET: Mister Foster, really! A married man. Look, Mister Flagg, a postcard. Shall I read it to you? "I'm covered in confusion"—and there's a funny man with no clothes on, all red because he's blushing.
"I'm covered in confusion
I'm a crazy goon

42

I forgot to tell you
To Get Well Soon—
Daddy-oh!"
Isn't that good? Who's it from, I wonder? Looks as
though they forgot to sign it. Still. You hold it like this . . .
(*Leaves the card in his hand, retains one letter.*)

FOSTER: He coming in, then?

ASH: I didn't expect it really. They're having a barbecue
at the school. He's got to be there, I accept that.

FOSTER: Yes.

(LAKE *comes on from left.*)

ASH: I shouldn't want him to miss it.

LAKE: That letter for me?

SWEET: Doctor Rees.

ASH: Nurse, I'd like to be moved into Kenneth's place.

SWEET: Mister Boyd's coming round now.

LOACH: Been coming for half an hour, me old mate.

ASH: Then afterwards.

LAKE: You ask Sister.

(*Loud burst of laughter and* BOYD *comes on in a dark suit,
escorted by* DR. BIRD, SISTER MCPHEE *and an* INDIAN
MALE STUDENT.)

BOYD: Good morning, Mister. How are your waterworks—
on the mend? (*Bends ear close to* FLAGG.) No good.
Can't hear you. What you in a cage for?

SISTER: Tried to get out, Mister Boyd.

BOYD: Tried to get out too soon, Mister. You might have
dropped a clanger.

(*Laughter from the* INDIAN STUDENT.)

All right. How's this embroidery? (*Examines* FLAGG.)
Not bad at all. Feel like getting up today? Have to
carry this bottle with you, all right? Well done.

(*Walks downstage with his party trying to keep up.* SWEET
moves in and tidies FLAGG.)

BOYD: Mister's had enlargement of the prostate, you
remember, with hesitancy of micturition, haematuria and

43

acute retention. I did a retro-pubic prostatectomy and Mister's got a self-retaining catheter in his bladder. Why, Mister?

(INDIAN STUDENT *racks his brains, vainly.*)

Miss Bird?

BIRD : So the nursing staff can check the amount of bleeding and obviate the danger of——

BOYD : And why do I want him on his feet so soon? Hurry up, because the post-operative problems are pneumonia and deep-vein thrombosis——

BIRD (*to* INDIAN STUDENT) : —leading to pulmonary embolus——

BOYD : —and he's enough to cope with as it is. The commonest cause of urethritis we should not consider at Mister's age. What's that, anyone?

(INDIAN STUDENT *racks brains.* DR. BIRD's *head nods forward.*)

Wake up, wake up——

(BIRD *brought to her senses, drops papers which* SISTER *and* INDIAN STUDENT *pick up.*)

A dose of clap! Then we might get stricture, retention, bladder hypertrophy, the whole caboodle. A warning to us all.

(INDIAN STUDENT *laughs again.*)

Not funny. Still, as I say, Mister's a bit past it. Mister Who, Sister?

SISTER : Flagg.

BOYD : Well, Mister Flagg's left that particular problem behind him.

INDIAN STUDENT : Mister Flagg's only at half-mast, eh, sir? (*No laughter.*)

BOYD : Are you disrespectful to the patients, Mister?

INDIAN STUDENT : No, sir.

BOYD : I hope not. Any questions? (*Doesn't wait for any but goes to between Beds 3 and 4.*) Where's Doctor Whatsisname?

SISTER : Last night, sir.

(*Whispers. He nods, turns at once to* LOACH. *Consults papers.*)

BOYD: Morning. They've found out who you are then.

LOACH: Yessir. Mister Loach.

BOYD: *Mister* Loach. We'll have to watch that.
(*Goes downstage again. They follow.*)
Mister's got brewer's measles.

BIRD: I thought he had a history of alcoholism, sir.

BOYD: Exactly, Doctor. Chronic gastritis, possibly cirrhosis.
Came in complaining of severe cramps and loss of
memory. The memory part's being looked at by the coppers
but what do you make of the cramps?

INDIAN STUDENT: Polyneuritis, sir.

BOYD: Hooray! Touch of foot-drop we might expect,
paraesthesia, formication—with an emm for anyone
about to laugh. Creepy crawlies.
(*Goes to* LOACH. *They all follow but* BIRD *who stands
dozing with her eyes shut.* SISTER *goes back and nudges her.
They join* BOYD *at the bed.*)
What's your poison, Mister?

LOACH: Brandy.

BOYD: Get cramps do you?

LOACH: Funny thing you should mention that. I do get these
what-I-call cramps like, in my leg.

BOYD: Have any trouble getting your foot off the ground?

LOACH: That's funny you asking that. I've said to the wife I
don't know how many times: I can't seem to get my
foot off the ground——

BOYD: Subject to wind?

LOACH: Like anyone, sir. Repeating.

BOYD: Open your mouth.

LOACH: Fouling the air.

BOYD: Open your mouth, I said.
(*He looks in, whistles in amazement.* INDIAN STUDENT
laughs.)

BOYD: You come to theatre tomorrow, I'll have a look at you.

45

LOACH: Tell you what, sir, I'll be all right now I know where I stand——

(*But* BOYD *has moved away already, The others follow as quickly as they can.*)

BOYD: Persuading him to take the cure, Doctor Bird?

(*She is the last to get there, having nearly dozed off again.*)

BIRD: Yes, sir.

BOYD: The houseman wants an oesophagoscopy?

BIRD: We ought to know what his insides are like.

BOYD: An illicit still, I should think. All right, what's an oesophagoscopy, Mister?

INDIAN STUDENT: Um—let me see now——

(*Thinks. Long pause.* BIRD's *papers drop from her hands.* INDIAN STUDENT *helps her pick them up.*)

BOYD: Never mind that.

INDIAN STUDENT: I had it on the tip of my tongue.

BOYD: Funny place for it. Usually down the throat.

INDIAN STUDENT: Of course.

BOYD: A tube down the oesophagus, taking care not to knock his teeth out.

(BOYD *goes to between Beds 1 and 2.* SISTER *has helped* BIRD *pick up papers again. Now she helps her stand.*)

SISTER: You all right?

BIRD: Long as I stay on my feet. I've been on duty for twenty-nine hours.

BOYD (*to* FOSTER): You one of mine, sir?

FOSTER: No, sir.

BOYD: Right, sir. (*to* ASH.) 'Morning, Mister, had enough milk pudding?

ASH: The mere sight of semolina makes me heave, Mister Boyd. Don't ask me why.

BOYD: Lovely grub. (*Scan's* ASH's X-*rays.*) How are you in yourself?

ASH: Not so dusty, sir, but then I never feel what-you-call on top of the world. My doctor wrote down all my symptoms, then he said "By George, you're a mess on paper".

BOYD: Worry about yourself?

ASH: I get depressed. I abhor my work.

BOYD: Find a hobby. (*Uncovers* ASH *and presses on his stomach.*) Take some interest. Brass-rubbing. (*Then brightly*): Basket-making.

(ASH *cries out.*)

Tell you what, your tummy's not much better. I want you in theatre tomorrow, do a bit of crochet-work.

ASH: *Physically* I'm not too bad, sir.

BOYD: Take away a bit of your stomach. You'll learn to do without it.

ASH: I thought I was on the mend.

BOYD: Much the best.

(*Moves down, they follow.*)

Mister's duodenal's failed to respond to a medical regimen. So what shall we do? Come on, come on, scream and hide our faces?

BIRD: Polya gastrectomy?

BOYD: At last. Of course he's a case, you can see that. Talk a gramophone to scrap by the look of him. Next, Sister? (*Takes papers, glances at them, makes for the right, saying as he goes*): Ah, morning, Mister. Bum any better?

(*And off, with* SISTER *and* STUDENTS.)

LOACH: You won't see me down no theatre. Soon as they bring me in my clothes, I'll be off. They can't keep me here against my will.

ASH: I thought I was on the mend.

FOSTER: He'll fix you up. You trust him.

ASH: Oh, he's a first-rate man, Mister Boyd. I'm taken aback, that's all——

LOACH: Is he a gen bloke, me old mate?

FOSTER: Harley Street.

LOACH: Go on——

FOSTER: We get the best here, don't you worry. All for the

47

price of a stamp.

ASH: No moving towards the balcony now.

LOACH: You can discharge yourself.

FOSTER: What for?

LOACH: I always been independent.

FOSTER: You can hardly move.

LOACH: Half these doctors, they tell you not to smoke, half the time they smoke more than what you or I do.
You look at Churchill.

FOSTER: Churchill wasn't a doctor.

LOACH: Never said he was.

(TYLER *comes from left in chair.*)

TYLER: Ready for the tea, Mister Ash?

ASH: Not today, friend. Got to rest. Major op. in the morning.

FOSTER: What's he got to do with it then?

(TYLER *rolls off right.*)

LOACH: Well, look at the way he smoked.

FOSTER: Yes, but he never told *you* not to smoke.

LOACH: No, but these doctors, *they* tell you not to smoke.

FOSTER: I never heard Mr. Boyd tell you not to smoke.

LOACH: Just let him try, that's all, me old mate.

FOSTER: He smokes a pipe.

LOACH: Next thing he'll be telling me to jack in the spirits.

ASH: Three weeks of tapioca—down the drain.

LOACH: Not bloody Russia.

FOSTER: You two need cheering up, taking out of yourselves.
Soon be T.V. time.

LOACH: Those blackies again, is it?

(*They settle to watch the play. Blue overhead light goes on for the night.*)

48

Lights dim on the ward but go on downstage.
Music.
NEIL *comes in with* STAFF. *He wears a suit and she a very revealing dress—low bodice and short skirt. Also far too expensive for a nurse.* NEIL *pulls up one of the armchairs from near the stove.*

NEIL: Come in, sit down. We'll have a wee dram.

STAFF: Is your father at home?

NEIL: Och, no. He's in Edinburgh giving a lecture on transplant techniques.
(*She sits. He leans over her.*)
What will you have to drink?

BARNET: His breath smelled fresh like pine. Cleo Norton's heart gave a painful jerk as his steely blue eyes met hers with a twinkle.

STAFF: Vodka and lime.
(NEIL *goes out of the light.*)

BARNET: She inhaled the masculine fragrance of the room. So this was the holy of holies, the inner sanctum!
(STAFF *stands again and walks about, looking at the room, objects, etc.*)
This was where Neil and his father had lived in bachelor splendour since his mother's death all those years ago. Every tiny thing was so male—the pipes in their racks, row upon row, the reassuring smell of Alsatian, the walnut shelves full of veteran car models . . . vainly Cleo tried to still the excitement that was making her breasts rise and fall like those of some love-sick teenager with her television idol.
(NEIL *comes back into the light, pushing a trolley with drinks. He gives her a glass of vodka.*)

NEIL: You enjoyed the concert then?

STAFF: Wonderful.
(*Turns back for his own drink.*)

49

BARNET: Yes, just as she'd enjoyed the village cricket-match, the rag ball and the Son-et-Lumière. But this was the first time she'd been brought home afterwards.

NEIL: Well—cheers!

STAFF: Cheers!

(*They drink.*)

BARNET: Perhaps the first night his father'd been away! Was he *ashamed* of her then? Or ashamed of what he meant to *do* to her?

(NEIL *smiles.*)

STAFF: So this is where you live in bachelor splendour.

NEIL: We've a dear old soul looks after us. (*Turns, puts down his glass.*)

BARNET: She pleaded with his grey flannel back: don't be like all the others. She was discovering that to say a girl was a nurse simply meant she was what the doctor ordered!

NEIL: Sit down, Cleo.

BARNET: She had given him no reason to expect anything of that kind.

(*She sits, exposing a lot of leg and bosom. He drains his glass, thirstily.*)

NEIL: So many evenings I've wanted to bring you back here.

STAFF: Oh?

BARNET: Her eyes urgently raked his face. Then why haven't you? She implored wordlessly. Perhaps your father doesn't approve of your seducing nurses?

NEIL: Only my father——

STAFF: Yes?

NEIL: Doesn't approve.

STAFF: I see. But you do?

NEIL: I approve of you, aye. No doubt about that.

STAFF: And of bringing me home to seduce me, because I'm a nurse—and a coloured nurse at that——

BARNET: She flared.

NEIL: Steady now——

BARNET: But the flood-gates were open now.

50

STAFF: —easy to use and throw away on the trash heap. Well —(*stands and moves to put glass on tray*). I'm not trash, Doctor Boyd. Your experienced eye has let you down tonight.

NEIL: You canna be serious——

STAFF: You can't satisfy yourself with me, then go and hold hands with Sister McPhee——

NEIL: Sister McPhee?
(*He has held her but now lets go and winces, his hand going to his back as he groans with pain.*)

STAFF: What's the matter? Neil!

NEIL (*recovering*): Nothing. It's nothing. Who told you that about Sister McPhee?

STAFF: Oh, it's common gossip among the nurses, you and Sister McPhee——

NEIL: Cleo, my mother always loved Mary McPhee. Her family lived in the next cottage along the glen. Her dying wish was that Mary should become one of the family (*takes her in his arms*).

BARNET: He drew her to him.

NEIL: What's more, my father believes only pain can come from trying to mix the races. He's no an evil man, you ken, but he doesna want to see you hurt. So I've been waiting——

STAFF: Neil!

NEIL: But I couldna wait any longer——
(*He embraces and kisses her.*)

STAFF: Neil——

BARNET: —She groaned, when his lips let her.

NEIL: I can't risk doing anything that would upset him. He's too valuable to society.

STAFF: And Sister McPhee—what about her?

NEIL: Mary's a friend of the family. That's all, as far as I'm concerned. But, Cleo, you and I—we're on the same wavelength——

STAFF: Honey——

51

BARNET: Hungrily his mouth sought hers——

STAFF: Wait. You better know. I won't be only a body to any man.

NEIL (shocked): No, Cleo, I'm in love with you.

STAFF: Maybe, Doctor Boyd, but you and I don't spell it the same way.

NEIL: Oh, we pronounce it a wee bit differently but we spell it the same.

STAFF: Don't try to be witty with me, Doctor. You spell it s-e-x.

NEIL: No!

STAFF: I'll never do anything dirty before marriage.
(*She turns her back and stands, legs apart, bosom heaving, hands on hips.*)

NEIL: It's not dirty. It's right and beautiful. How can I make you understand that?
(*From behind he kisses her neck and shoulders.*)

BARNET: She could smell the sweet, hot, peppermint cleanness of his breath.

NEIL: We've started something we're going to have to finish.

STAFF: Oooh . . .

BARNET: His lips trailed fire . . . a warm sweetness was suffusing her thighs——
(BOYD *has entered up the front stairs.*)

BOYD: Good evening.

BARNET: They spun round.

NEIL (*turning*): Father!
(*In his spin, he falls, winces, seizes his back. He suffers a spectacular paroxysm.*)

BOYD: What's wrong, son?

STAFF: Neil what is it?

NEIL (*gritting his teeth*): It's nothing . . . nothing, I tell you . . .

BARNET: They stared at each other—wordlessly.
(*Lights fade. Music. Black.*)

The spot searches the stage and finally finds BARNET, *pushing on his trolley.*

BARNET (*to* SPOTMAN): Better. (*Looks at trolley, whips off cloth.*)
A woman's work is never done. Look here—shaving
brush, some lathery soap, a mug of hot water, an old
strop and a cut-throat.
(NURSES *are seen in the light spilt from the spot. They
come on and prepare* ASH *for operation, putting on a white
smock, etc.*)
Not that it's going to get near many *throats* today.
Quite the reverse—all right, màdam, we know you're
always the first to savvy smut. Nothing to be proud of.
They'll laugh at anything, some people. This has got to
be done. Not to make them beautiful, no, it's sanitation.
(ASH *wheeled forward in bed so that he is between*
BARNET *and* AUDIENCE. *As one of the* NURSES *passes*
BARNET, *he gooses her with the shaving brush. She makes
shocked face.*)
Thank you, ladies. Now let's see—(*lifts bedding to expose*
ASH *to him.*) Lie on your right side. Now relax. I know
it's difficult, you naturally tend to recoil from anything
nasty—unlike some I could touch with a very short
stick——
(*Glances at* WOMAN *in* AUDIENCE. ASH *makes indistinct
comments and sounds during this monologue.* BARNET
lathers brush and then ASH's *stomach.*)
Which is why I try to keep talking, take their minds off
it. If it's a Jew, I might ask for the loan of a fiver and that
so frightens him I get on better. Now the the man who
used to do this job—well, it wasn't so much a *job* to him,
it was a labour of love! We used to issue tin trousers
whenever he was on duty. No—hospital barber, very
good at short-back-and-sides, but they took him off

pre-operatives. They had to, after a patient complained
he'd had his privates shaved when he was only going to
have his tonsils out. (*Starts to strop the razor.*) Personally
I thought it was a shame. I sympathize with the customer,
yes, and Vernon never learnt to hide the pleasure it gave
him. But. It's not a vocation many are drawn to and most
of the healing arts are bent if you want my frank opinion.
(*Begins shaving.*) Now don't flinch or you'll do yourself
a mischief. I've no idea what your convictions are about
this highly controversial issue. You were a teacher, that's
the same country. A socially acceptable sublimation.
Take this case described in a medical journal I bought one
afternoon in Soho. This poor berk said to his
psychiatrist, he said, Doctor, Doctor, I've got a problem;
I find I only fancy thirteen-year-old boys. So the Doctor
said, Well, everyone to his taste, it's tricky but not in-
superable. And the patient said, yes but only thirteen-
year-old boys with a wet chest cough. And, d'you know,
it was enough for him to *hear* them cough. Now I'm
going to ask you to hold your own, if you'd be so kind.
Down out of the way, you've got the idea.
(*Goes to shave, reacts to* AUDIENCE *with arch disapproval.
Then shaves.*)
Anyway, d'you know how they fixed him up? He's a
voluntary health visitor to the children's ward of a large
London chest hospital! Welfare work combined with
harmless pleasure, the secret of a happy life. But because
poor old Vernon overstepped the mark, he's probably
up the West End every night exposing himself to all and
sundry . . . I've no idea what your views are but I feel a
useful person should not be made a scapegoat because
of one misdemeanour . . . did I tickle? I sometimes think
I should charge. Never mind. All over now and very
comical you look, if you'll pardon my saying so.
(*Covers* ASH *and turns him on his back. Another* ORDERLY
has come on, smoking a cigarette, reading a paper and

pushing a stretcher trolley.)
Hullo there, Michael, top of the morning to ye.
(MIKE *coughs in reply, continuing to smoke. They lift*
ASH *from the bed on to the trolley.*)
How about Minestrone in the two-thirty at Chepstow?
(MIKE *coughs again, pausing to recover.* BARNET *makes
long-suffering face at* AUDIENCE. *They carry* ASH *to the
stairs on the left and begin the descent.* LAKE *has joined them
with* ASH's *charts.* SWEET *and* SISTER *upstage have moved*
FLAGG *along to replace Bed 4: put* ASH's *empty bed in
Position 5. As* MIKE *and* BARNET *begin to go down,* ASH *is
severely tilted and* MIKE *has another fit of coughing. They
pause while he recovers.*)
Look at it. The International Passport to Smoking
Pleasure.
(LAKE *takes the cigarette and stamps it out.*)

LAKE: One day you'll drop somebody.
BARNET: Don't you say that, nurse. He's worked for all the
   big construction firms, haven't you, Michael? Up the
   ladders. MacAlpine . . . Wimpey . . . you know what
   Wimpey stands for? We Import Millions of Paddies Every
   Year . . .
   (*They descend out of sight.*)
   (SWEET *and* SISTER *have been getting* FLAGG *out of bed.*
   SWEET *carries a drainage bottle attached to* FLAGG *by a
   tube. They walk him to the armchairs and settle him in
   one.* SWEET *stands the bottle beside him. During the scene
   that follows it slowly fills with urine.*)
FOSTER: Good old Dad! That's the way!
SISTER: Isn't he a clever boy!
   (FLAGG *speaks to* SISTER *but she has to bend over him to
   hear.*)
   I don't know what the physiotherapist would say, I'm
   sure, but—Mr. Foster, can you let him have a cigarette?
FOSTER: Certainly. Help yourself, Dad——
   (SWEET *gets them and gives one to* FLAGG.)

55

SISTER: Light it for him.
> (SWEET *lights it, puts it in* FLAGG's *mouth. He manages to smoke it by concentrating hard.* FOSTER *and* LOACH *cheer.*)
> Clever's not the word.

LOACH: I could do with a smoke meself.
> (SWEET *returns cigarettes to* FOSTER. LOACH *touches her arm*)
> I say, I could do with a smoke meself, me old mate.

SISTER: You're on your way to theatre, Mr. Loach, and Nurse Sweet is not your old mate.

SWEET: Thank you, Mister Foster.

SISTER: Mister Foster, keep an eye on this sprightly lad. If there's any change in the colour of the fluid, call a nurse. Understand?

FOSTER: Sister.

SISTER: There's an ashtray. Come along, Nurse.
> (*She and* SWEET *go off left.* FOSTER *laughs.*)

FOSTER: Talk about tore you off a strip.

LOACH: Right. That's her lot. I got her number. She's for it.
> (FOSTER *laughs again.*)

FOSTER: Your face!

LOACH: They pick on a man when he's helpless. Shit-scared.

FOSTER: What you scared of?

LOACH: Theatre. I never asked to go to no theatre.

FOSTER: It's only an examination.

LOACH: *They* say. Once they get you on the table, how you going to stop them? Lady friend of mine, they give her the jab, when she woke up, d'you know what they'd bloody done to her?

FOSTER: What?

LOACH: Took a breast off.

FOSTER: She must have signed a form.

LOACH: They give you a form to sign, how d'you know what you're signing? I signed a form but they don't tell you all what's in it. All the small print. Can't read it, half the time.

FOSTER: Perhaps you should have glasses.

LOACH: They'd like to see me in glasses, some of them. And dentures.

(FOSTER *laughs.*)

That's all right, me old mate, you have a laugh on me. About all I got left to give you.

(BARNET *and* MIKE *have come up the other stairs with the empty stretcher. They put it on the trolley and wheel it to* LOACH'*s bed as* SWEET *comes back.*)

BARNET: Bring out your dead! Bring out your dead!

LOACH: Here, Michael, got a drop of brandy on you, me old mate?

SWEET: That's enough of that, Mister Loach.

(FOSTER *laughs.*)

LOACH: He likes a laugh at me, old Kentish Town here.

SWEET: Ups-a-daisy.

(*They put him on the stretcher.*)

LOACH: Anything to do with operations, know what I mean, nurse?

SWEET: You'll be getting a pre-med injection downstairs.

LOACH: What, a jab? Needle in my arm?

(*They put him on the stretcher and wheel him to the stairs.* SWEET *brings charts.*)

BARNET: Or your bum.

LOACH: Anything to do with needles . . .

SWEET: Try to relax now.

LOACH: Drop of ether . . . go down nicely. . . .

They go out of sight, MIKE *coughing.*

Pause.

FLAGG *smokes.* FOSTER *watches.*)

FOSTER: Alright, Dad? . . . Want any help?

MACKIE: He's barely conscious. Can't even hear you.

FOSTER: Doing well though. I never thought to see him up again. The will to live, it is. My dad's the same. Eighty-two and game for anything. I say All right, Dad, Woburn Abbey! Up he gets, puts his mac on, always first in the minibus. Rhine Valley, the Riviera; Yugo-

57

slavia last year. Mother's dead so we take care of him.
He's less trouble than one of the kiddies.

(SISTER *returns, takes* FLAGG's *cigarette and stubs it out.*
FLAGG *seems to be dozing. She checks the bottle.*)

SISTER (*loud*): Having forty winks?

(*No answer. She goes off right.*)

FOSTER: During the season we go most Sundays, perhaps as
far as Beaulieu for the veteran cars or Longleat, Dad
likes the lions. Picnic in the car park or on the lawns,
where there's an eating enclosure. If it's wet, we most
likely nip out to Hampton Court, have a laugh at the
maze. I'm more interested in the history side myself.
I like to get by the guide and pick his brains. Or sometimes the owner's doing a stint—some duke or marquis
—and I think to myself: your days are numbered, old
son. All these fallow deers and statues are going to be
taken over by the state—not before time either—and
you will have to buy your ticket with the rest of us.
(*He lights a cigarette.*) I find a special interest in the ser-
vants' quarters. I say to the wife, you'd have been here,
love, a skivvy for life, and I'd have been one of an army
of gardeners scything the lawn from dawn to dusk. But
these lords are only holding on by our permission and
when they've served their purpose, they'll be out. Not
that I've anything against them personally but we're not
living in the Dark Ages with Queen Victoria sitting in
state. This is the twentieth century, d'you agree?

MACKIE: The armies of democracy on the move.

FOSTER: Pardon?

MACKIE: Columns of minibuses . . . moving up the motor-
ways . . . from Hampton Court to Woburn Abbey . . .
Woburn Abbey to Windermere——

FOSTER: Why should they have it all to theirselves?

MACKIE: —a world of lay-bys, drive-ins, pull-ups . . .

FOSTER: Better than when my Dad was a boy, never got his
nose outside the street he——

58

MACKIE: You a Socialist?

FOSTER: I'm a Socialist, yes, I'll be quite frank with you.

MACKIE: Not a Communist?

FOSTER: No fear. I don't agree with extremes. Let the Communists try to come in here, I'll fight to keep them out.

MACKIE: Why?

FOSTER: Well, for a start, they've done away with religion, haven't they.

MACKIE: You religious?

FOSTER: Personally no. I only ever go in church to see the stained glass—but I don't reckon you should do away with anything just because you don't believe in it. That's the meaning of freedom, live and let live.

MACKIE: The early Socialists thought . . . if we achieved this, the rest would follow.

FOSTER: Achieved what?

MACKIE: This state we're in. This ward. Where men are prevented from death by poverty or curable sickness even the least intelligent . . . least healthy or useful . . .

FOSTER: You've got to do what you can for people——

MACKIE: Can't cure loneliness—boredom—ugliness . . . but at least you can see they're lonely on clean sheets . . . ugly on tapioca pudding . . .

FOSTER: Why can't you try to look on the bright side?

MACKIE: I'm dying of a stomach cancer and the pain's only bearable with pethedine and morphine. I've asked them to let me die . . . but because of their outdated moral assumptions they have to keep me going——

FOSTER: Isn't life precious, though?

MACKIE: *Good* life. Useful life. Good *death's* precious too, when the time comes. If you can get it. My heart's stopped once already, which used to be called death . . . now they bring you back . . . I've had it written in my records: don't bring me back again.

(BARNET *and* MIKE *come from below carrying* ASH. LAKE

59

carries his drip and drain. MIKE *is coughing. He has to pause.*)

BARNET (*to* AUDIENCE): There's a requisition in for a lift.

LAKE: Has been for years.

BARNET: We'll never get it, unless we let somebody fall.

(MIKE *recovers and they climb.*)

They say there's been a bit of everything on this ground —a priory, a bowling green, a jail, Methodist chapel, workhouse. The present structure's a fever wing, put up to house the cholera victims. None of your modern rubbish, mind you. Built to last. It will too!

(*They reach the top and take* ASH *to his new bed place in the corner.* LAKE *attends to his drip.* BARNET *speaks to the ward in general.*)

Old Boyd has tasted blood this morning. Like a butcher's shop down there——

(FOSTER *laughs.*)

SISTER (*coming on and cutting* BARNET *off*): Thank you, Mister Barnet.

BARNET: Thank you, Sister. The surgeon looked at his list of operations: this lot now and after dinner four abortions. He said to me: It's Murder Mile. All morning we save the old, all afternoon we kill the young.

(*He and* MIKE *go off downstairs with their empty stretcher.* SISTER *checks* FLAGG's *bottle then helps* LAKE *with* ASH.)

MACKIE: This fellow's returned to go. And Flagg's gone up one. They don't even bother to move me any more——

SISTER: Sing a different song, Mister Mackie.

MACKIE: At least you've shown you don't expect me to last much longer.

FOSTER: Good job we don't all talk like that, eh, Sister?

MACKIE: In lucid moments, I like to talk. My only remaining pleasure.

FOSTER: Not much pleasure for the rest of us, eh, Sister?

SISTER (*going to* MACKIE): Come on, cheer up, use your earphones.

MACKIE: Oh, good God! (*He almost laughs but it starts a cough. A short one.*)

SISTER: Wouldn't you like a chat with the Chaplain?

MACKIE: I parted company with organized religion some years ago . . . when I saw it was being used to justify the activities of cretins . . . Jesus Christ lived in a largely unpopulated world . . . disease and natural hazards killed off multitudes every year . . . kept the balance of nature . . . if He came back today, He wouldn't say, "Thou shalt not kill", He'd advocate mass euthanasia . . .

SISTER: We can't estimate the value of a life.

MACKIE: Time we could. Not enough kidney machines, someone's going to have to . . .

SISTER: I'm not going to stand here listening to all this childish nonsense.

MACKIE: If somebody doesn't let us die—or prevent others being born—there are going to be seventy million British by the turn of the century——

SISTER: I shall get you a sedative.

(*She goes off.* LAKE *deals with* ASH.)

MACKIE: And thirty million cars . . . this sceptr'd isle with its rivers poisoned . . . beaches fouled with oil . . . the sea choked with excrement . . . the polluted air alive with supersonic bangs . . . that what you want? The Socialist Nirvana?

FOSTER: You're a whining Winnie, I know that.

MACKIE: But—abortion—euthanasia—birth control won't be enough . . . some government will have to have the guts to stop people coming in . . . filling the country——

FOSTER: Nurse, nurse! The bottle.

(*Points at* FLAGG. LAKE *goes to look and finds some blood in the urine.* SISTER *comes back.*)

MACKIE: Enforced emigration too . . . fill the empty spaces in Australia, Canada . . . manpower must be directed where it's needed . . .

SISTER: Better let him have a rest.

(*She and* LAKE *help* FLAGG *back to bed.*)

MACKIE: Break the power of the unions and make people do what they're told . . . close down the luxury trades, put a stop to gambling and vice . . . send the croupiers to work in penal colonies . . . get the striptease girls back to the farms . . .

(BARNET *and* MICHAEL *bring* LOACH *up the front steps, with* SWEET *attending. Take him to Bed 3.*)

BARNET: Can't hear yourself think down there for the squeak of rubber gloves.

MACKIE: Because, you see, it's not only a question of the natural resources of the land . . . there's a spiritual cancer too . . .

BARNET: Dear oh Dear! She sowing discontent again?

MACKIE: A nation doesn't grow great on material greed without a sense of duty . . . Churchill knew this, he got the best from us, inspired us with purpose. . . . National Service turned boys into men . . . the world's finest youth club——

(*Slowly lights go down on the rest of the ward and only* MACKIE *remains lit. In the darkness,* LOACH *and* FLAGG *are settled and* BARNET, SISTER, SWEET, MICHAEL *and* LAKE *go off.*)

—but now the Chatterley Set are destroying our moral fibre with liberalism . . . fornication . . . paederasty, drug-taking condoned by the Church . . . remember the fall of the Roman Empire, as Mr. Carson of Woolwich Holdings was saying to me . . .

(LAKE *comes on with a hypodermic. She cleans his arm. He doesn't notice her.*)

Mixed marriages advocated on television . . . which God never intended . . . proved scientifically that some races are genetically inferior . . . no good sullying sound stock with an alien strain . . . jazz dancing and——

(LAKE *injects a sedative.*)

—factory farming . . . but first—let the old go . . .

62

give us the gas chambers and we will finish the job . . .
(LAKE *has gone. A hand bell tinkles.* SISTER *comes on
ringing it and all available* NURSES *and* ORDERLIES *bring on
vases of flowers as the light grows to a warm summer
evening.*)

SISTER : Ready for visitors?
(*And the* VISITORS *come, from up the front stairs and from
the right. Most of them go through the ward and out to
the left.* TWO WOMEN *sit at* FLAGG *and* FOSTER's *beds.*
MACKIE *sleeps.* ASH *and* LOACH *read, eat fruit, etc.* LAKE
*comes on with a trolley of tea and begins giving cups to
those patients who can drink.* SISTER *looks at the effect.
It satisfies her. She nods at the* AUDIENCE *and goes off right.
It looks like a flower show.*)

ACT TWO

Scene One

A front cloth representing the end wall of the hospital. An open doorway cut in it allows us to see the ward behind. Four armchairs facing the AUDIENCE.

ASH is in one, working on his basket, LOACH *in another, reading* Daily Mirror. MACKIE *is propped up in an invalid chair.* ASH *has a white creamed face.*

Long wait, then LOACH *looks up*

LOACH: Here—Cambridge.

ASH: Why d'you call me that?

LOACH: Eh?

ASH: Cambridge.

LOACH: Anyone that reads a lot I call Cambridge.

ASH: I see.

LOACH: What's that noise?

ASH: Didn't notice.

LOACH: Like a Siamese cat.
    (*They listen.*)
    There!

ASH: Oh! A baby.

LOACH: Go on.

ASH: In the premature unit.

LOACH: What, came too soon?

ASH: Yes.

LOACH: Babies over there . . . cemetery behind the car park . . . I don't know.

ASH: There's your National Health, friend. Look after you from the cradle to the grave.

LOACH: Marvellous, isn't it? Ah! Sod it!

ASH: Pardon?

LOACH: Got the cramps. I thought that surgeon was going to fix me up, get rid of these sodding cramps . . . then I come round—what's he done? Took a couple of teeth out. Who asked him?

ASH: Friend, they were rotting in your head.

LOACH: My business if they were. 'Twasn't a toothache I came here with. I came in here with my memory. Police brought me in. Found me wandering.

ASH: Well, you know who you are now.

LOACH: Edward Loach.

ASH: Know who your wife is?

LOACH (*takes out snapshot, looks at it*): Not looking forward much to her coming in.

ASH: She's frowning in the sunlight, that's all.

LOACH: She's always frowning, me old mate, wet or fine. I like a laugh and a joke, that's only human nature, isn't it? She's a good woman, I don't mean that. Keeps a good house. But always on at me to take the cure. *They* better not start . . .

ASH: You *should*. It's your only feasible course.

LOACH: I shall turn round and tell them what to do with it. Down the country, miles from civilization. You wouldn't knob it!

ASH: But you must rest, in any case.

LOACH: Rest? Couple of mates of mine went in for it. They told me what a rest it is, thanks very much.
(*Rubs his leg, wincing.*)
Course, I *used* to drink for pleasure. I'm going back a few years now. Lately it's more like you might say medicine. Used to get *drunk* too. Used to be drunk days on end. I don't reckon there's nearly so much pleasure taken nowadays in getting drunk. Not like there was.
(FLAGG *arrives, walking with two tridents, attended by* NURSE LAKE. *He no longer has a drain bottle.*)

65

ASH: Here we are then——

LOACH: Hullo, Dad.

LAKE: What d'you think of him?

ASH: Like a two year old.

LAKE: Soon be bringing round the tea.

ASH: We'll take it round together. I had to drop that job
for a few days.

(FLAGG *is put into a chair.* LAKE *goes.*)

LOACH: I was laughing then. I'm talking about Shanghai.
Beach-combing I was in the International Settlement.
You ever been Shanghai way?

(ASH *shakes his head.*)

China way? Hong Kong. Kowloon Ferry. Only cost you
a ten-cent piece in the days I'm talking about. Ship
Street? With all the girls hanging in cages? So you could
pick them out before you went in for your jig-jig.

ASH: Poor creatures.

LOACH (*shrugs*): All they're used to, isn't it? They haven't
been civilized. Some are all right. The Gurkhas, now
you're talking. Good little fighters. Always give you a
salute and call you sahib. Knew their place. Tikh-hai,
Johnny. Give them a couple of chips, your slave for
life. Salaam, sahib. I was a sort of batman to the engineers.
Slept out on the beaches, never knew a day's pain.

(FLAGG *has been struggling to take a letter from his
pocket. He holds it towards them.*)

FLAGG: I heard from my brother this morning.

ASH: *Did* you, sir? Well done, well done!

(*They tend to shout at him as if he were foreign.*)

FLAGG: Tells me he's just had a letter . . . posted 1943 . . .

ASH: *Go* on.

FLAGG: 1943 . . . now . . . to post a letter then cost . . . two-
pence halfpenny—right?

ASH: Right.

FLAGG: So the post office want him . . . to make up the dif-
ference . . .

66

ASH: Up to fourpence? A penny halfpenny.

FLAGG: Penny halfpenny . . . but they reckon it was under-
paid by the sender . . . so they're asking for double . . .

ASH: Threepence?

FLAGG: For a letter sent in 1943!

ASH: And delayed by the Post Office?

LOACH: Bloody marvellous, isn't it?

FLAGG: Course . . . he's going to fight it.
(*Leans back, exhausted.*)

LOACH: Only right.
(*They watch as* FLAGG *nods off.* ASH *fiddles desperately
with his basket.*)
I was a sort of batman to the engineers. Where I learnt
my trade of catering. Africa this was. You ever been
Africa way?

ASH: Never that far afield.

LOACH: I know Africa like the back of my hand. Stopped
at a place half-way to Khartoum. Tents is all it was.
Miles from sanitation. Nothing to drink but minerals
and half the time they blew up before they was opened.
And class distinction! Wouldn't look at you, the British
civvies. I turned round to one of them, I said, look, me
old mate, we're not wogs. I said, it's not for *me* Mac-
Alpine's building the sodding pipeline. Educated
people treating us no better than blacks.

ASH: We're all brothers beneath the skin, friend.

LOACH: That's what *I* said. I said, we're all British and
the British ought to stand together against the wogs.
Perhaps if we had, we might still have the Empire, right?
But it's like I say, these doctors just the same. They turn
round and tell you to jack in smoking, half the time
they're smoking more than what you or I do.
(LOACH *lights cigarette.*)
My smoke's the only friend I got. It is. I used to have
some good old mates. If they was alive to see me now,
in this condition, they'd drop dead. A man needs a

67

mucker, I don't care what you say.

ASH: That's true. I certainly——

FLAGG: What day is it?

LOACH: What d'you say, Dad?

FLAGG: What day is it? Is it wrestling?

LOACH: Coronation Street today. Isn't it, me old mate?

ASH: I believe so.

LOACH (*loud, to* FLAGG): Coronation Street. Seen the paper? (*Gives him* Daily Mirror. FLAGG *nods and reads.* LOACH *smokes.* MACKIE *groans in his sleep. They look at him.* ASH *suddenly loses control and throws his unfinished basket off the stage, down between the flights of stairs.*)

ASH: Perishing basket! It's a losing battle. Physio-therapy. Physio-fiddlesticks!

LOACH: Easy.

ASH: How is basket-making supposed to help the frustrations of a lifetime? (*Sits again.*) When I was forced to give up teaching, I had a mental breakdown. They made that an excuse for getting rid of me, but it was they who'd caused it. In fact, I'd have to lay my perforated ulcer directly at their doorstep.

LOACH: Go on.

ASH: If you pushed me.

LOACH: Where was this?

ASH: In Bristol.

LOACH: What?

ASH: My home town.

LOACH: Chew Stoke?

ASH: You know it then?

LOACH: Chew Magna?

ASH: Just outside.

LOACH: I could have played tennis in Chew Magna. (ASH *tries unsuccessfully to construe this.*)

ASH: I suppose what got me through was the thought of my adopted boy. My wife couldn't have children. We're separated now, it never went too swimmingly. I was awarded custody.

LOACH: Was it to do with her underneaths?

ASH: I'm sorry.

LOACH: To do with her womb, was it?

ASH: Yes.

LOACH: Womb trouble.

ASH: That sort of thing, yes.

LOACH: Mine's the same.

ASH: Still. The time seems to have come when he's ready to go on his own way. Looks as though I shall be left on my lonesome. Which is when I shall be glad of the belief in reincarnation I drew from my study of Comparative Religion. The belief that we can store up character in life after life until we attain perfection.

(LOACH *feels called on to speak but finds nothing.*)

Childish weakness, I dare say, but there, I take after mother, she was the timid one. Father was like a lion, with all the faults of the lion too. Proud, unapproachable, mean-tempered. I revered him. I had to find a source of strength to replace him when he passed on. A steadfast faith. (*Puts his hand on* LOACH's *knee.*) People like us need a crutch to help us.

LOACH: I never been a church-goer.

ASH: That makes no odds. People with dependant natures, we have to draw our strength from where we can. Help each other.

LOACH: Man needs a mucker.

(ASH *nods.* FOSTER *arrives, with* LAKE *assisting.*)

ASH: Hallo, Desmond. What you doing running about?

LOACH: Running about now.

LAKE: There you are.

LOACH: Old Kentish.

(FOSTER *sits in remaining chair.* LAKE *looks at* FLAGG.)

LAKE: This patient all right?

FLAGG (*opening eyes*): Dinner already?

LAKE: No, not yet. You all right?

(FLAGG *nods.*)

All right, that patient?

(*She looks at* MACKIE, *who stirs and nods.*)

FOSTER: Thank you, Nurse.

(LAKE *goes.*)

You noticed that Nurse never knows anyone's name?

LOACH: Marvellous, isn't it?

FOSTER: What?

LOACH: Typical.

FOSTER: They reckon she's the best in the ward.

(FOSTER *watches* LOACH *closely.*)

LOACH: That's obvious, isn't it? You can see that.

(ASH *has moved to edge of stage. Shouts down.*)

ASH: Friend, I wonder can I trouble you to throw up the basket?

(*It is thrown from below. He catches it.*)

Ta very muchly.

FOSTER: How's your tummy, Mervyn?

ASH: Not too bad, what remains of it.

FOSTER: Kept your breakfast down?

ASH: Boiled egg, yes. My aim now is to work my way back to the semolina.

FOSTER: And the eczema?

ASH: Oh, under control, yes.

FLAGG: Look at this, Alice. This young hussy showing all she's got.

LOACH (*nervous*): Who's Alice?

FOSTER: His wife. (*To* FLAGG.) All right, Dad.

(FLAGG *looks at him, then goes on.*)

FLAGG: Seen this young tart here, showing all she's got?

FOSTER: Not bad at all.

FLAGG: Sixteen, it says . . . I'd give her sixteen, if she was one of mine . . . never seen Alice undressed all the years we've been together . . . our young days, no decent couple . . . would have had connection before marriage . . .

FOSTER: Time Marches On.

FLAGG: You what?

FOSTER (*shouting*): I say, Time Marches On.

FLAGG: Yes.

(*Closes eyes and rests.* LAKE *returns with bottles.*)

LAKE: Who wants a bottle?

LOACH: Depends what's in it, eh, me old mate?

(LAKE *reaches under* FLAGG'*s blanket and puts a bottle there, replacing a full one.*)

Drop of three-star go down very nice.

ASH: Sssh.

LAKE: This patient want a bottle?

(MACKIE *looks at her, shakes his head. She goes.*)

MACKIE: I drift off and nearly sleep and one of these happy days I shan't come back.

ASH: Now, now . . .

MACKIE: But someone's always calling me back for a cup of tea or . . . a bottle . . . an overdose of the right drug is what I want.

LOACH: Whining Winnie's off.

MACKIE: Well, what are *you* hanging on for? You've been saying you've nothing to live for but your cup of tea . . .

FOSTER: We want a lecture, we'll ask for one.

ASH: Try to count your blessings.

MACKIE: You count them. I'm too busy coping with the pain . . . they wouldn't kill a pig like this . . .

ASH: Human life and a pig's life——

MACKIE: I've no regard for life itself, only the quality of life . . . should be clinics where you could get your death as you get a library book——

FOSTER: Tell us the same old story.

MACKIE: The Eskimos let their old die in peace.

FOSTER: The Eskimos haven't got a health service.

MACKIE: Learn a lot from primitive people . . . or old civilizations . . . I was an engineer in India . . . Burma . . .

LOACH: I was a sort of batman to the engineers.

MACKIE: Some remote station, under canvas . . . the bull-

71

frogs barking in the dark . . . I'd walk by the water . . .
hear somebody drumming . . . singing . . . I was a father
to those people and I learnt from them as you learn from
children . . . a world thrown away by a nation bent on
suicide . . .

FOSTER: Hullo!

MACKIE: . . .too many rats will tear each other to pieces . . .
and on the roads or in the air . . .

(FOSTER *has begun the Gaumont British theme song
again. The others join in,* LOACH *tone-deaf.*)

the urge to self-destruction is given official sanction . . .
kill yourselves and leave the country to the mental
defectives . . . the senile . . .

(*He is beaten by the singing, and has to leave off but his
effort to raise his voice has brought on a spasm of acute
pain. For a few moments the others sing on but his groans
become cries.*)

ASH: Nurse! Call the Nurse!

FOSTER: Nurse!

LOACH: Nurse! Come on, me old mate.

(SISTER *comes from the ward.*)

SISTER: What is it, Mr. Mackie? Want a lie down?

(SISTER *begins to wheel him off.*)

Don't want to cry now. Frighten the other patients . . .

(*She wheels him off.*)

FLAGG: What's the matter with him?

LOACH: Nothing, Dad. You read the paper.

ASH: Poor fellow.

FOSTER: I've no patience.

ASH: Oh, Desmond.

FOSTER: All right for him going out to India, lording it. But
I'm not sorry the Labour Government gave it back to
its rightful owners. We're better off without all that.

ASH: Oh, yes, but I meant Mr. Mackie's suffered more——

FOSTER: No, we could all look on the dark side. I could have
let this dicky ticker get me down but soon as I grasped

72

I'd have to curtail my summer plans I said to the wife:
No Costa Brava for us, love, not this year. So we shall
manage with day trips. Some of our nicest holidays were
during my shifts at country junctions—I'm a signalman.
Park the bus and the boys and I pitch the tent in the
nearest field, Grandpa get the Volcano going, soon have
a decent cup of tea. Mother give our youngest the
breast . . . I join the boys in a game of cricket between
trains. What could be nicer?

ASH: You're a lucky man.

FOSTER: I know it too. Five lovely kiddies. My eldest girl,
she's six, she looked at me, you know the way they do,
very threatening, I thought hullo, what have I done
now? She said to me, Daddy, you're the only one who
hasn't waggled my loose tooth.
(*They all laugh.*)

ASH: Mackie's case is different.

FOSTER: Granted.

LOACH: What's he got, Cambridge?

ASH (*almost a whisper*): Cancer.

LOACH: Get out.

ASH: Oh, yes.

LOACH: That what the smell is?

FOSTER: But you look at Mr. Tyler. (*To* LOACH.) Diabetic
in the wheel-chair. Nine times in here in the last two
years and every time an amputation. First his toes, then
his feet, then his legs——

LOACH: All right, me old mate.

ASH: Wonderful spirit!

FOSTER: There you are. Life and soul. And always busy with
something useful.

ASH (*nodding*): Last few days he's been learning Mah Jong.

FOSTER: Always a joke. They say you can hardly get out of
bed, when you get back in he's put a bedpan in it.

LOACH: Got to keep smiling.

ASH: But highly intelligent people can be more sensitive.

73

FOSTER: They've got no right to be.

ASH: Take my brother. Brains of the family, a chartered accountant, he got hold of some poppycock about there only being so much energy and we mustn't squander it. Started sleeping all day and staying awake at night, drawing off terrestrial dynamism. Finished up in a mental home, writing notes to nurses rather than speak —please let me have a bottle—rather than waste his store of energy. Raving bonkers. I worshipped him.

FLAGG: Brought some rhubarb, Alice.

(*They all look at him.*)

LOACH: All right, Dad?

FLAGG: I like a bit of stewed rhubarb, plenty of sugar. Fresh from my allotment.

LOACH: Very nice.

(*Silence again.* FLAGG *looks at his paper.* ASH *fiddles with his basket.*)

Those premature babies . . . don't half make some bloody ugly noises.

ASH: Can you blame them?

(LAKE *and* BARNET *come on, bustling.*)

BARNET: Come on, ladies, bustle, bustle!

LOACH: What is it now then?

BARNET: Matron's rounds.

FLAGG (*brought to his feet by* LAKE): What's up?

LAKE: Got to see Matron.

LOACH: Marvellous, isn't it?

FLAGG (*going off*): Visiting, is it? Visiting time?

LAKE: Matron.

BARNET (*to* ASH): Come on, Pagliacci.

LOACH (*laughing*): Pagliacci!

BARNET (*to* AUDIENCE): Something to pass the time.

(*The patients hobble towards their beds as the cloth goes up to show the ward.* BARNET *clears their chairs.*)

74

SCENE TWO

Bright light.

The five beds are as they were: FOSTER, LOACH, FLAGG, ASH *and* MACKIE. *As* BARNET *moves across with the chairs,* SWEET *comes from left.* MACKIE *groans.*

SWEET: All right, Mr. Mackie, Doctor's on the way. Try not to make a fuss while Matron's here.

BARNET: He ought to be moved out.

SWEET: Wait till Doctor's seen him.

BARNET: Right . . .

LAKE *leaves* FLAGG *and goes off right with* SWEET. BARNET *leaves chairs at stove and turns as* MATRON *comes from right, with* SISTER, LAKE *and* SWEET *attending. She is regal, smiling, but wastes no time.* BARNET *goes off left.*)

MATRON (*to* MACKIE): Good morning, how are you today?

(*Groan of agony from* MACKIE.)

Keep smiling. You'll soon be out of here.

(*Moves to* ASH.)

MATRON: Good morning, how are you today?

ASH: Morning, matron, not so dusty, thank you——

MATRON: That's the style——

ASH: When you consider half my tummy's been——

MATRON: Keep it up.

ASH: —taken away.

(MACKIE *groans. Everyone looks at him, except* MATRON.)

MATRON: Good morning. How are you getting along?

FLAGG: Eh?

MATRON: Are they treating you well?

FLAGG: Not too bad.

MATRON: That's right.

FLAGG: Though I'd like to go to a toilet—you know——

MATRON: Sister——

FLAGG: —toilet with a decent chain.

75

MATRON: Get this patient a bedpan.

SISTER: Nurse Lake——

LAKE: Sister?

SISTER: Get Mr. Flagg a bedpan.

LAKE: Nurse Sweet——

MATRON: Good morning, how are you?

LAKE: Get Mr. Flagg a bedpan.

LOACH: Well, miss, I get these cramps——

MATRON: (*looking at her watch*): Good.

LOACH: In my leg.

SWEET: Mister Barnet——

MATRON: Soon be out of here.

LOACH: I don't want the cure.

BARNET (*coming on left*): Hallo?

SWEET: Bedpan for Mr. Flagg.

BARNET: Right. Morning, matron.

MATRON: Good morning, how are you getting on?

FOSTER (*without removing earphones*): Lovely, Matron, everything's lovely——

(BARNET *has gone off right.*)

MATRON: That's what we like to hear, isn't it, Sister? Get well soon. We need the beds.

(*Goes off, left, with* SISTER *and* LAKE. SWEET *breaks off, as* BARNET *re-enters, right, with a bedpan for* FLAGG.)

BARNET: You couldn't have waited, could you?

FLAGG: What's this?

BARNET: Get the screens.

(*He and* SWEET *go off, right.*)

FLAGG: What's he brought me this for?

ASH: You said you wanted to go to the toilet.

FLAGG: No.

ASH: I heard you.

FLAGG: She said, "Are you all right", and I said, "All right but I'd like a toilet with a decent chain . . . like I got at home . . ."

(BARNET *and* SWEET *return with screens, erect them around*

FLAGG's *bed.*)

ASH: Mister Flagg doesn't want a bedpan. He only said he was looking forward to a toilet with a decent chain.

BARNET: Do us a favour, Mary Pickford. Matron says "Do this", it's the Royal Command.

(*They go behind the screens and we hear them.*)

FLAGG: I don't want no bedpan——

SWEET: Come along, Mister Flagg——

BARNET: Knickers down—and——

SWEET: Ups-a-daisy! There.

(DR. BIRD *comes from right, checking papers, looking about, as dazed as before.*)

BIRD: Mister Mackie?

FOSTER (*taking off earphones*): By the door, Doctor.

(BIRD *goes to* MACKIE, *checks his chart. He groans. She glances at him and goes on with the chart.* SWEET *and* BARNET *come from* FLAGG's *screens. Look up the ward to see where* MATRON *is.*)

SWEET: Where's Her Majesty?

BARNET: On the balcony.

BIRD: How d'you feel?

(SWEET *now notices* BIRD.)

SWEET: Ah, doctor.

BIRD: Nurse, this patient should have the screens round.

SWEET: Right. (*To* BARNET.) Get more screens for Doctor.

BARNET: They're all being used—up there, look!

(MACKIE *cries out.*)

BIRD: Nurse!

SWEET: Yes, coming.

(BARNET *shrugs, rolls one of* FLAGG's *screens away and puts it upstage of* BIRD, *so that we can now see* FLAGG *unnaturally high on his bedpan, as well as* BIRD *with* MACKIE.)

LAKE (*off*): Mister Barnet!

BARNET: Coming!

(*Goes off left.* BIRD *begins an examination of* MACKIE,

77

refers to his chart, listens to his chest. Her head remains
there. SWEET *meanwhile has shuffled the chairs about*
near the stove, keeping a nervous eye on MATRON'S *progress.*)

SWEET: Shall I take you off, Mister Flagg?

FLAGG: I never wanted to come on here . . . but now you
   better leave me.

SWEET: Oh.
   (*Goes to* MACKIE'S *screen and peers round the edge. Sees*
   the DOCTOR'S *head on his chest. She nudges her awake.*)
   Doctor!

BIRD (*waking*): —we'll aspirate a pleural effusion——
   (*The movement has hurt* MACKIE, *who cries out.* BIRD
   stands.)
   Oh, yes. Thank you, nurse.
   (*Leads* SWEET *from screens to centre stage.*)
   He should be in the terminal ward. Ask Sister to
   arrange it. I'll be with the almoner if you want me——
   (*Finishes in an irrepressible yawn.* SWEET *nods and goes*
   to move the screen back to cover FLAGG. BIRD *wanders*
   towards the left.)

FOSTER: Whoa, doctor! Other way if you're going out.
   (BIRD *turns yawning. She makes for the right, dropping*
   papers all the way. SWEET *picks them up and sticks them*
   back under her arm as she goes off. BARNET *comes from*
   left.)

BARNET: She's coming down the other side.
   (SWEET *returns to meet him.*)

SWEET Mister Mackie to the terminal ward.
   (*Together they wheel* MACKIE'S *bed into the centre, then*
   back through the exit right.)
   Go for a nice long ride now, Mister Mackie?

BARNET: Chuff-chuff-chuff-chuff whoooooweee!
   (*And off, as* MATRON *comes from left with* SISTER *and*
   LAKE.)

MATRON (*looking at her watch*): Those chairs are anyhow,
   Sister, put them straight.

78

SISTER: Nurse Lake——
>   (SWEET *comes back and begins rolling* MACKIE's *locker off,*
>   *right.*)
LAKE: Sister?
SISTER: Those chairs are anyhow.
LAKE: Nurse Sweet——
SISTER: Put them straight.
>   (BARNET, *returning, takes the locker off and* SWEET *joins*
>   *the* MATRON's *party in time.*)
LAKE: Those chairs are anyhow.
SWEET: Mister Barnet——
LAKE: Put them straight.
>   (BARNET *returns.*)
SWEET: Those chairs are anyhow. Put them straight.
>   (BARNET *shuffles the chairs about.* MATRON *comes down-*
>   *stage, speaks to* AUDIENCE.)
MATRON: We're removing the beds as they fall vacant because,
      I'm glad to be able to tell you, the whole ward block
      is in for a very extensive face-lift. Which I am sure you
      will agree is long overdue. The walls will be in washable
      avocado pear, the curtains and counterpanes in
      Cotswold Stone. High level louvres on the windows.
      King's Fund Beds with Slimline mattresses.
>   (*She turns to survey the ward and to imagine this*
>   *transformation.* SISTER, LAKE, SWEET *and* BARNET *do the same.*
>   *Appreciable pause.* FLAGG *farts and groans. No one*
>   *acknowledges it.* MATRON *turns back, smiling.*)
      Into the jet-age with one big jump. (*She crosses to*
      right, notices MACKIE's *bedspace.*) Another one gone there,
      Sister?
SISTER: Um—it looks like it.
MATRON: Good, good. Keep them moving.
>   (*Goes off, right, with* NURSES *and* BARNET. FLAGG *does*
>   *it again.*)
LOACH: Dear, oh Lord!
ASH (*amused*): Musical evening.

79

(FOSTER *takes off his earphones.*)

FOSTER: Her Majesty gone?

LOACH: She's gone, yes.

ASH: Desmond, I've just this minute noticed something.

FOSTER: What's that, Mervyn?

ASH: I'm in the end bed.

(*They look. They see that this is true. They find nothing to say.* BARNET *comes on downstage with trolley. Spot finds him.*)

BARNET: Running spot man? You wouldn't know a running spot if you had them all over you. At the end, Mr. Mackie's heart stopped three times and three times they brought him back. They were fetching the artificial respirator when it stopped again and some daring soul decided to call it a day. (*Peers in at the end of the cover. Pauses, speaks more quietly, not facing the* AUDIENCE.) I'm sure I speak for all those who knew him in life when I say that he will be remembered as an evil-tempered, physically repulsive old man. The distended lips, the purple ears, those malevolent eyes glaring up at you from the engorged face. But—now the pump's been allowed to pack up, the flesh has receded, that puffiness gone, an altogether younger face has appeared. You can see how—once—someone might even have fancied him. (*Looks at* AUDIENCE, *then pushes trolley off other side.*)

SCENE THREE

Music.

Lights change to a brilliantly lit downstage area. The setting cool and white with fixed wash bowls and gadgets dispensing toilet requisites.

BOYD *comes up front steps in light, white clothing—cap, boots, trousers, short-sleeved shirt. He takes own pulse rate. Goes down on his hands and does a few press-ups. Holds up one hand to check its steadiness.* SISTER MCPHEE *comes into the area, wearing white theatre gown.*

SISTER: Mr. Boyd.

BOYD: Ah, Sister—they're ready?

SISTER: Ready and waiting, sir.

BOYD (*he begins to wash his hands*): And—Neil?——

SISTER: There's been no change.

BOYD: And—the donor?——

SISTER: Staff Nurse Norton is ready.
    (BOYD *stops washing his hands.*)

BOYD: Aye, she's ready. Ready to give a kidney to save my
    son's life.

SISTER: Aye. Because she loves him. Because her life wouldna
    be worth living without him.
    (*He goes on washing. She looks at him.*)
    I know how she feels.
    (BOYD *stops again, looks at her. With his elbow he
    operates a nail-brush dispenser, taking the brush with
    his other hand and using it to continue washing.*)

BOYD: Mary—I wish I knew what to say to comfort ye. I
    tried—God knows I tried—to make him leave the girl.

SISTER: No!

BOYD: Aye, the girl who's about to risk her life that he may
    live.

SISTER: No.

BOYD: Aye. And whose fault is it his disease is so advanced?
    Mine.

SISTER: No.

BOYD: Aye!

SISTER: You mustn't ever think that, even for a moment.

BOYD: Why not? It's the truth, woman. I told him I wouldna
    speak to him again, until he'd broken it off with Staff
    Nurse Norton.

SISTER: No!

BOYD: Aye!

(*He finishes washing, throws brush into pedal-bin which* SISTER *opens with her foot and closes with a clang. He holds out hands for towel. She takes one from the sterilising unit with forceps and puts it into his hands. He dries hands.*)

Why else d'you think he didna speak to me of the pain he must have been suffering? And the worst of it was I never let on to mesel what my real motives were. I thought the odour of sanctity was in my nostrils and all the time it was the stench of racial prejudice.

SISTER: No.

BOYD: Oh, aye. I was a pig-headed old fool. I ken well.

(*Drops towel into receptacle. He takes folded gown and flicks it open, easing into it, touching it as little as possible with his hands.*)

And, Mary, I told mesel I was doing it for you. I promised Flora on her death-bed that you should be Neil's wife . . . and I did my best to see that you were.

SISTER: But Neil doesna love me.

BOYD: I've told him he wants his head examined. If you loved me as you love him——

SISTER: But I——

BOYD: And if I were thirty years younger—I'd not stand havering here like some timorous sawney——

SISTER: But I don't love Neil. I never have.

BOYD: Urmph? Have a care what you say, woman.

(*They move towards each other from opposite sides of the room. As they are about to meet——*)

SISTER: Age has nothing to do with love.

(*He turns his back to her and she ties the laces behind his gown. They play the next dialogue in that position.*)

BOYD: D'you know what you're saying, woman?

SISTER: Oh, aye. I've had thirty years to learn the truth of it. To be near you yet far from you. I never dared to hope . . .

82

BOYD: D'you know what kind of man you'd be getting? An old fool who thought he could play God?

SISTER: No!

BOYD: Aye! Who thought he could tell people whom they should love. Who thought he knew the score but who wasna so canny as a wee bairn.

(*He turns to her and their eyes meet.*)

SISTER: No.

BOYD: Aye! And who couldna see what was before his verra nose. (*Holds out his hands towards her.*) Mary——

(*She presses a button which squirts a jet of powder upwards into his hands. He rubs them together as she moves further away. Then he follows her.*)

SISTER: Who was the only man with the skill to save his son's life!

BOYD: No!

SISTER: Aye!

(*They stop face to face with a machine between them. She presses a switch with her foot. A packet of rubber gloves pops up from the machine like bread from a toaster.*) Staff Nurse Norton could give Neil her heart well enough but without your help she couldna give him her kidney.

(*He takes and flicks open the packet of gloves, then puts them on. He presses his palms together in an attitude of supplication and keeps them so for the rest of the scene.*)

BOYD: Great surgeons are two a penny . . . but a good woman . . . can you ever forgive me, Mary?

SISTER: Oh, dearest——

(*He closes his eyes and raises his face towards her. At the touch of another switch a theatre mask springs up. She takes it and puts it over his mouth.* LAKE *has come on and ties the laces behind his head. He opens his eyes and looks at* SISTER.)

Good luck—sir.

(*He nods, turns and goes towards the darkness, his hands*

83

pressed together, as though to prayer. SISTER *and* LAKE *follow.*
Music swells.)

Lights brighten the ward.
SWEET *comes from right briskly.*

SWEET: Walking patients up now. Rise and shine.
  (*Goes off left.* ASH, LOACH *and* FLAGG *climb out of bed and come down to the stove and its chairs.* FLAGG *has a paper,* LOACH *a cigarette.* FOSTER *remains in bed, his eyes closed.*)
LOACH: Get up, lay down, drink this, swallow that . . . marvellous, isn't it?
ASH (*smiling*): The well-nigh inexplicable rituals of our confinement, friend.
LOACH: And what have they done? Time slipping away, all they can think to do is bang me knees with little hammers and come round half a dozen times a day for a sample of my blood. It's not *their* time, is it? It's mine. And time's money, I don't care what you say.
ASH: I wish mine was.
LOACH: Any more doctors come round me for blood, I shall turn round and ask them straight what they're doing with the bleeding stuff?
ASH: They're students, practising.
LOACH: I shall say: what you doing with it, drinking it, are you?
ASH: Perhaps they're testing the alcohol content.
LOACH: Chance'd be a fine thing. I was gonna get Joyce to bring me in a drop when she come, just to soothe the cramps sort of style. But now she've gone off like

84

that, shouting the odds, I don't reckon on seeing her
back . . .

ASH: Why don't you take the cure, Ted?

LOACH: Middle of visiting too . . . no consideration—keeps a
clean house, you follow my meaning, but nervous.
Over-sensitive.

ASH: Forgive my saying so, she seemed to like showing
off.

LOACH: Not the first time she's left home. Mind you, we
haven't *got* a home, she's down the Centre. We had a
very decent little room in this condemned terrace,
soaking wet but independent, you follow me. But now
she says the Council's pulling it down. I saw the rent
tribunal, they say you've paid your rent, you stay where
you are. Still, time I get out of here, it might be a
flyover. How can I stay where I am when it's gone?
If I hadn't lost my memory, I'd still be in possession.
Nine points of the law. Fellow in our place, they said
we'll put you in the Centre and like a fool he went.
Now what he *should* have done, he should have let his
wife and kids go in the Centre but *he* should have stood
still. In possession. Get a place much quicker if they got
to turn you out. So they *say*. There again, you never
know. One says one thing, one another. (*Winces with
cramp.*)

ASH: We're in a very similar boat.

LOACH: You got your adopted boy.

ASH: Got him? Where? Where is he? Has he come to visit
me?

(SWEET *returns from left.*)

SWEET: Come on, Mister Foster, put those earphones away.
Time to stretch your legs.

(*Goes off right.* FOSTER *takes no notice.*)

ASH: No. My boy doesn't want me now.

LOACH: You haven't got my craving. My cramps.

ASH: I've a nervous temperament, my mother's legacy. Only

half a stomach . . . nervous eczema.

LOACH: Good job——

ASH: Ha!

LOACH: Education.

ASH: Well——

LOACH: Always been my handicap, no education. Take those school magazines you give me to read. I couldn't keep up the interest, see. Where you could.

ASH: Education's wonderful, that's true.

LOACH: Educated people always got the whip hand.

ASH: You remind me to count my blessings, friend. Though, of course, many so-called educated people are no better than you or I when it comes to being a Good Samaritan.

LOACH: Oh, definitely. Those sahibs down Khartoum way treating us no better than blacks.

ASH: I'm grateful to you, Ted, for pointing out the glint of sunshine in an otherwise impenetrably murky sky. That's the beauty of having a friend to talk to.

LOACH: Man needs a mucker——

ASH: My name's Mervyn.

LOACH: —don't care what you say.

(ASH *puts his hand on* LOACH's *knee.*)

ASH: Thank you, Ted.

(*From the right now enters a* WEST INDIAN CLERGYMAN *in the most gorgeous vestments the Anglican Church allows for administering the Last Unction. The* PATIENTS *look up at him. After his impressive sweeping entrance, he falters and consults a card. He then goes to* ASH's *bed and checks his chart.*)

Can I help you, Chaplain?

CHAPLAIN: Ah. I'm looking for Mr. Mackie.

ASH: I'm afraid you're out of luck.

CHAPLAIN: What ward is this?

ASH: Sir Stafford Cripps.

CHAPLAIN: Yes. I've got Mister Mackie down for the end bed.

LOACH: He's dead.

CHAPLAIN: Ah.

ASH: Passed on the night before last. In the terminal ward.

CHAPLAIN: Oh, dear, somebody slipped up on their paperwork. Too many cooks spoil the broth. (*Writes on the card
he brought and puts it away.*) Get my breath back a moment.

ASH: Too much red tape in your department too, Chaplain?
(CHAPLAIN *sits between* LOACH *and* FLAGG.)

CHAPLAIN: I'm afraid we've a very severe attack of Parkinson's
Law.

ASH: Same everywhere.

LOACH: Mate of mine had that.

CHAPLAIN: Pardon?

LOACH: Nasty.

CHAPLAIN: Parkinson's *Law*.

LOACH: Shaking and falling about.

CHAPLAIN: Seen the papers this morning?

ASH: Oh, yes.

CHAPLAIN: Pretty shocking news.

ASH: It is.

CHAPLAIN: England are going to have to pull their socks up
to make a hundred between them. Bad generalship.
Same old story. They used to say the British Army
in Fourteen Eighteen were lions led by lambs and it's
the same story at Lords. Haven't I seen you at
Communion?

ASH: Yes, Chaplain. Ash the name.

CHAPLAIN: Ah, yes. Sorry I haven't popped in sooner but,
as I say, no rest for the wicked. I was giving the last
unction to a patient in Sherpa Tensing ward and thought,
while I was in this neck of the woods, I'd . . . kill two
birds with one stone. I mean, by having a natter with
Mr. Mackie. Was he C. of E.?

LOACH: The way he talked, he had no time for religion.

CHAPLAIN: Ah, well, they always put C. of E. for that.
Saves a lot of paperwork. No, I was afraid it was going

87

to be some mistake I'd have to spend the rest of the day putting right. We're snowed under with paperwork.

(*Pulls up the hem of his cassock and gets packet of cigarettes from jacket pocket. Offers them.*)

D'you use these fellows?

ASH: I won't now, thank you.

LOACH: Don't mind. Thanks, Johnny.

FLAGG: I'll have one.

(CHAPLAIN *looks for lighter in pocket, then gets attaché case and opens it on his knees.*)

CHAPLAIN: You know, the great juggernaut of bureaucracy grinds to a halt. Only yesterday I was called to the intensive care unit to give Communion to a Palestinian Arab.

(*Laughs. From the case he takes a candlestick with candles, a spotless linen altar-cloth, a bottle of wine, a cup and paten and a prayer book. He sets them in turn on the floor.*)

A Moslem, needless to say. Still he was a very decent sort. The Holy Land used to be my stamping-ground in Forty-Four Forty-Five. . . so he put me in the picture on my old haunts. . . .

(*Finds lighter and uses it. They smoke. They help him put the articles back into his case. They smoke again.*)

No, it's the same old story, I'm afraid. A lot of first-rate players don't make a team without the leadership.

(*The* OLD WOMAN *in the flowered dress has entered. She goes to* FOSTER.)

LOACH: Same old story, isn't it?

CHAPLAIN (*enthusiastically*): That's it exactly.

OLD WOMAN: Good morning, I have a message for you. God so——

(FOSTER, *still with earphones, does not wake. She is very slightly disconcerted to be talking to herself, but she puts a text between* FOSTER's *fingers as his hand lies over the counterpane. The men downstage have been embarrassed by her arrival, largely on the* CHAPLAIN'*s behalf. She now comes to them.*) God so loved the world that He gave His only begotten Son that whosoever believeth in Him should not perish but have everlasting life. (*She notices the Vicar's vestments. She smiles uncertainly and goes off left.*)

CHAPLAIN: *And* it looks like being an all-Australian Wimbledon again.

LOACH: Marvellous, isn't it? We used to lick the world at one time.

FLAGG: See in the paper where they're trying to bring back capital punishment.

CHAPLAIN: Ah?

FLAGG: Bring back hanging . . . some member of Parliament . . . they come round in my street . . . petition . . ..

CHAPLAIN: Yes.

FLAGG: List of signatures . . . wanted me to sign to bring back hanging . . . I said: No fear . . .

CHAPLAIN: Did you?

FLAGG: No fear, I said . . .

CHAPLAIN: Well done!

FLAGG: I said: Hanging's too good for them. They ought to be slowly tortured to death . . . any ruffian that has a go at a little girl or police constable . . . ought to be taken limb from limb, I said . . .

CHAPLAIN: I don't know that I could altogether agree with that. (*Smiles at them all.*) Not altogether.

ASH: Nor I. I don't believe in cruelty.

CHAPLAIN: Quite.

ASH: They should be strung up. It's quick and merciful.

CHAPLAIN: So many different sides to every question. (*Stubs out cigarette.*) Well, I must love you and leave you. At least a dozen bods in this ward marked C. of E. Most of them turn out to be Greek Orthodox, I daresay. (*Looks at card again.*) Mister Mackie, yes. Mister Ash —wasn't it?

89

ASH: Yes, Chaplain.

CHAPLAIN: And you're Mister——

LOACH: Loach.

FLAGG: Flagg.

CHAPLAIN (*ticking names*): Wonderful. Now. Mister Foster——

ASH: Having forty winks.

CHAPLAIN: Better have a word.

ASH: Let me bring you a chair. You're not allowed to sit on the bed.

(CHAPLAIN *and* ASH *go to* FOSTER'*s bed,* ASH *bringing an upright folding chair.*)

CHAPLAIN: Oh, yes, we don't want to break the rules. These nurses put the fear of *God* into me.

(*Laughs and sits, as* ASH *goes to his own locker and gets his basket.*)

Come along, squire, wakey, wakey.

(*Shakes* FOSTER *to wake him. He falls sideways, his head lolling over, the phones still on.* CHAPLAIN *pushes back chair, stands.*)

Mister Foster—(*he has to support the falling body.*) Nurse! Sister! I'm afraid this patient doesn't seem too well . . .

(*The* PATIENTS *stand and move as* SWEET *comes on from right. She looks at* FOSTER *briefly, feels his pulse. She looks at the* CHAPLAIN, *then tries to go off the way she came.* LOACH *is in the way.*)

SWEET: You patients, back into bed, please! Out of the way.

SCENE FIVE

The PATIENTS *go back to the beds.* SWEET *goes off right very quickly.* CHAPLAIN *looks again at* FOSTER, *then at his list, then goes off left to his next patient.*

SWEET (*amplifier*): Stafford Cripps here. I've got a cardiac arrest B for Bertie. Thank you.

(*Meanwhile* LAKE *and* BARNET *bring on screens to part-conceal* FOSTER.)

BARNET: (*to* PATIENTS, *as he adjusts screens.*) Why don't you listen to the wireless? Much nicer.

ASH: Not working, Mister Barnet.

BARNET: Watch the telly then!

(SWEET *comes back with tray of apparatus and goes behind screens. We see the nurses pull back bedding and* SWEET *attempts mouth-to-mouth ventilation.*

Light fades on this and a large acting area, coming in from above, lights the down right section. Lift comes up with two operating tables on it, attended by white-garbed figures. The PATIENTS *are covered but their feet are bare: a black pair and a white.*

Music; Romeo and Juliet Overture.

The ATTENDANTS *wheel the tables to directly beneath the acting area. Behind the tables, a wall is flown in, white-tiled but having on it twin anaesthetic machines, X-rays, Oscillographs. Other* ATTENDANTS *wheel on instrument trolleys, wash-bowls, etc. The operating staff are masked and wear white boots.*

BOYD *comes up front steps, sideways, still in his attitude of prayer, followed by* SISTER MCPHEE, *as before.*

Their movements are ritualistic but played too much to the gods.

BOYD *approaches* CLEO's *table, looks at* ANAESTHETIST, *who nods decisively.* BOYD *turns to* MCPHEE, *holds out hand for first instrument. The other members of the team close in in and hide the operation from view at the very moment when it promises to be interesting. Music stops.*

Our attention is drawn to FOSTER's *bed by one of the screens being pushed over on to* LOACH.)

LOACH: Here!

(BARNET *comes out and pulls it straight as* INDIAN

STUDENT *hurries on from right pushing Cardiac Arrest Trolley, with Oxygen cylinders.*)

BARNET: Where've you been—up The Khyber Pass?

INDIAN STUDENT: I was in the canteen.

(BARNET *allows him behind screens. We hear the following dialogue, or some of it, very quiet and natural.*)

SWEET: I've tried mouth-to-mouth ventilation.

INDIAN STUDENT: No joy? We better do some external cardiac compression.

LAKE: On the floor, don't you think? The bed's too soft.

(*They lift* FOSTER *off the bed and lay him on the floor downstage of the bed,* BARNET *trying to hide all this from the other* PATIENTS *with screens. The* PATIENTS *try to concentrate on the Kidney Transplant.*

DR. BIRD *comes up front steps, wearing ordinary clothes with a raincoat, which she is taking off. She gives it to* BARNET *as she goes to help with* FOSTER.)

INDIAN STUDENT: We've tried mouth-to-mouth——

BIRD: Give him oxygen.

(LAKE *turns to trolley and searches.*)

BIRD: I was just off home for an hour's sleep.

LAKE: Sorry.

(*She walks swiftly off to the right as* BIRD *crouches over* FOSTER *and presses his chest.* BARNET *closes it off with screen and comes to us.*)

BARNET: Typical balls up. No spanner for the oxygen cylinder. Always the same—people don't put things back where they found them. Talk about a Band of Hope Concert.

(MICHAEL *comes from right pushing Defibrillator on trolley.*)

That's the Rescuscitation Unit.

(*Another man follows and* LAKE *now returns with the spanner.*)

With the aid of cardiac massage and electric shock, they've got a very creditable record of bringing them back from over the Great Divide.

(*They both go behind the screens and close off our view. Music and the lights come up on transplant.* SISTER *turns from her position beside* BOYD *and checks her instruments. As the light favours her face,* BARNET *moves across down-stage, bringing a hand-mike from the wings and stands near her.*)

In the terrible loneliness of the operating theatre,
so many times she had stood beside him, this grizzled
man with the strangely tender eyes, whose love she
had never dared to crave.

(*She turns back to hand* BOYD *an instrument.*)

So often she had tried to anticipate his every movement,
deftly slipping the instruments between his gloved fingers.
But this was no common-or-garden kidney transplant. A
glint of panic deckle-edged the usually inscrutable features
of the man who was trying to save the life of the boy who
had carried her satchel all those years ago.

(BOYD *stands up decisively, the kidney is lifted in a sterile bag and* BOYD *steps clear of the scrum. The scrum moves across to* NEIL's *table.* BOYD *comes to* MARY *and washes his hands of blood. She mops his brow.*)

Above the mask, her eyes met those of the man who,
in a rare moment of candour, had freely admitted that
he was not God.

(*He nods formally and moves back to the other table. Mary stands behind him.*)

A cavorting lancet of pity stabbed her behind the
sternum. She wanted to tell him: never mind, never
mind. . . .

(*Lights and music out.*

At FOSTER's *bed, the same clumsy movements and the same attempts to conceal them. They have got* FOSTER *back on to his bed.* BARNET *goes across downstage.*)

All going well as can be expected but not so nice for the
other patients. Which is where the telly is a great step
forward. Keep their minds off what's going on next

door. One of the problems here is not knowing how long he'd been away. Or where.
(Screens open to allow MICHAEL *to come out with Defibrillator.* BARNET *goes on, to himself.)*
Excuse me, sir, I understand you've just come back from that undiscovered country from whose bourn no traveller returns?—That's correct, yes. Now, as this is going to be an increasingly common experience in the years to come, I wonder if you'd say a few words about The Afterlife? And keep it short, we're running late.
*(*BIRD *and* INDIAN *have come out and go off right.* SWEET *has wheeled off cardiac arrest trolley.* FOSTER *has been got back into bed again. There is a noticeable lack of urgency about these movements.* BARNET *stares at them and glances at the audience, awkwardly smiling. From the left, on his level, the* OLD LADY *returns from her tour of the ward.*

OLD WOMAN: Good morning, I have a message for you. God gave His only begotten Son that whosoever believeth in Him should not perish but have everlasting life.
*(*MICHAEL *has returned pushing the hooded trolley. The* OLD WOMAN *gives* BARNET *a text and he goes up to assist in getting the trolley through the screens to* FOSTER. *The* OLD WOMAN *goes off down left, crossing the transplant area.*
Music and lights on OP.
BOYD *raises his head to the* ANAESTHETIST, *who gives thumbs-up. The scrum parts to allow* BOYD *to emerge. Music triumphant. He goes to instruments trolley and removes gloves.* MCPHEE *takes and throws them on to tray. He removes his mask. The* ATTENDANTS *are wheeling away the* PATIENT *and the rear wall is flown. Before the instruments trolley is wheeled off,* SISTER *takes* BOYD'*s pipe from under a white cloth and puts it into his mouth. Together they circle and he partners her in a pirouette. They dance off as the music ends.*

94

Lights off on Op.
FOSTER's screens part and are removed by LAKE and SWEET.
MICHAEL and BARNET begin pushing the hooded trolley off
to the left. The CHAPLAIN has come on and has to pause
while they pass.)

BARNET: Missed the boat again, Chaplain.

(CHAPLAIN *wanders forward, taking out his list and*
scanning the names. LAKE and SWEET return and wheel
FOSTER's bed off to right.)

LAKE (*as she passes*): Foster. C. of E.

CHAPLAIN: Ah!

(*Crosses off FOSTER's name and follows his bed out.*
ASH, FLAGG and LOACH watch silently as SWEET returns
and removes FOSTER's locker and earphones.)

SCENE SIX

Strong daylight.
A large Negro ORDERLY wheels on a trolley with a game set on
it. ASH, LOACH and FLAGG have climbed out of bed and are putting
their gowns and slippers on.

ORDERLY: All right, here?

LOACH: Tikh-hai, Johnny.

(ORDERLY *goes off, left. LOACH, ASH and FLAGG draw up*
chairs and settle round the game.)

He's new.

ASH: He's a prince, they tell me The son of a chief.

LOACH: Where's he from then? Africa way?

ASH: More than likely. If I remember correctly, it was
friend Flagg's throw.

(FLAGG *throws dice.*)

95

LOACH: Every time anyone comes in, I'm shit-scared they're going to want me for the cure. I'm all booked in. I've heard of this place and all. Down in Kent, a mile's walk from a Green Line bus.

FLAGG: Piccadilly with two houses.

ASH: That's your own.

FLAGG: Right . . .

(LOACH *throws dice.* FLAGG *looks about.*)

Another scorcher.

ASH: Makes you glad to be alive, this weather.

FLAGG: We could use the rain.

ASH: *You* could perhaps.

FLAGG: Soil must be parched.

LOACH: Bleeding Chance.

(*Takes and reads a card.*)

FLAGG: Son-in-law's looking after my allotment . . . well as he can . . . never had the feeling for it . . .

LOACH: Pay School Fees of a hundred and fifty pounds. Marvellous, isn't it?

ASH: You get two hundred for passing Go, so here's a fifty.

(ASH *throws a dice.*)

Have you always had green fingers, Mister Flagg?

FLAGG: Come from the country in the first place.

ASH: Did you?

FLAGG: Hertfordshire. Before my family settled in Islington.

LOACH: Never had much time for the country.

FLAGG: Then, of course, my job . . .

ASH: Free parking. What *is* your job?

FLAGG: Trees in streets . . .

ASH: Your throw.

FLAGG: Parks department . . . for the council . . .

LOACH: *I* been with the Parks department.

(FLAGG *in the act of throwing, looks at* LOACH *sceptically, then throws.*)

LOACH: In my trade of catering. Well, I looked after the chalet while the rangers were out on patrol picking up the soiled French letters.

FLAGG: What for?

(FLAGG *has taken a card*.)

LOACH: My job, wasn't it? Custodian of the chalet. Making the breakfast.

FLAGG (*gives card to* ASH *to read*): No, why'd they pick up the French letters?

ASH: Annuity Matures. Collect one hundred pounds.

LOACH: This was in Hyde Park I'm talking about. The tarts used to do their business in the spinneys . . . overnight this was . . . and leave this muck laying about.

ASH: Your throw, Ted.

LOACH (*throwing*): We tried putting barbed wire round but the ponces must have had cutters. Next day the rangers'd find this way cut through and all the used French letters again. What's this—Bow Street.

ASH: Mine. With four houses. Seven hundred and fifty pounds.

LOACH: Where'm I going to get my hands on seven hundred and fifty pounds?

ASH: You'll have to mortgage, Ted.

LOACH: I'm bloody mortgaged already, aren't I? Look at that—Mayfair and Park Lane, mortgaged. Even mortgaged the stations. I'm jacking it in. (Moves from table.) (*The Negro* ORDERLY *crosses left to right carrying a bedpan covered with a cloth.* LOACH *looks up at him, frightened.*)

I thought he'd come for me.

ASH (*approaching him*): Don't throw in the sponge, Ted. You can owe it to me.

LOACH: I don't want to play the bleeding game. It's a kid's game.

ASH: You can't sit day after day waiting and worrying. You must fill in the time.

LOACH: I'm all shot to pieces. How can I settle me mind to anything? Bottle of Hennessy and I'd be laughing . . .

ASH: Now come on. You promised me. What did you

promise? That you'd summon up your courage and face the cure. Then, once you're better—and it won't take long, you're half-way there already—then you'll come and lodge at my place and I shall help you to keep the pledge. And I can. I'm strong when it comes to helping others. (*Pause.*) All right, Ted?

(LOACH *nods.* ASH *sets his chair straight and* LOACH *sits in it.*)

My throw. Forget the rent. The important thing is to keep the game going. Regent Street. My own.

(ASH *pays him.* FLAGG *throws.*)

FLAGG: But say what you like, there's nothing finer than a fresh English tomato . . . plenty of salt . . . fresh pulled lettuce . . . crisp white heart . . .

ASH: Two hundred pounds for passing Go. To him that hath it shall be given.

(BARNET *has come on, pushing bottle trolley.*)

BARNET: This ward's a dead-and-alive hole. Time something happened.

LOACH: Jesus God, I thought you'd come for me. For the cure.

ASH: Don't tell me it's got *you* down, Mister Barnet.

BARNET: Long as trade's brisk I don't mind . . . but this——? Beds disappearing . . . gives you the creeps.

LOACH: I see you got a new wog helper.

BARNET: Prince Monolulu? Yes.

LOACH: Worming their way in. Another bleeding Chance, look at that.

BARNET: When he's carried the bedpans for a couple of weeks, he's going back to Timbuktu and run this brand new hospital they're building.

LOACH: Get out of jail free.

ASH: I told you things were looking up. You stick with me, Ted, we'll be all right.

BARNET: You could have done with that before.

LOACH: I keep it, don't I?

BARNET: Couldn't you, me old mate? Done with it before?

LOACH (*to* ASH): Your go.

BARNET: D'you get many pouffes in prison?

LOACH: Who told you anything about me being in prison?

BARNET: You did.

LOACH: In confidence.

BARNET: Funny places to put a pouffe, though, when you think of it.

FLAGG: Best place for them.

BARNET: D'you think so, Dad? I find that interesting, that point of view.

FLAGG: Give them the cat.

BARNET: Hear that, Ted? The cat. They might enjoy it, though, a few of them.

ASH: Bang on Go. That's lucky for me.

BARNET: You've got to be so careful you don't give people pleasure.

LOACH: Some of the types I saw in there, I thought to myself this is a waste of the ratepayers' money.

(FLAGG *throws and moves.*)

BARNET: I think they can be useful members of society, long as they sublimate their libidos. Look at male nurses.

FLAGG: You're a male nurse.

BARNET: I'm an orderly, thank you. No connection with the firm next door, Fairies Anonymous. Ballet dancers. Scout masters. Teachers. There you are. Teachers! We had a master when I was a kid, name of Nash, we called him Nance. Everyone knew but him.

ASH: I bet he did know.

BARNET: What?

ASH: His nickname. You always do. The boys think you don't but you do.

BARNET: Did you know yours?

ASH: Cinders.

BARNET: Short for Cinderella, was it?

(*Winks at* LOACH, *who does not see, busy throwing the dice.*)

ASH: No. (*Laughs.*) A play on words. My name Ash, you see. Cinders—Ash.

BARNET: I'm with you now, yes. Clever, eh, Ted?
(*Nudges* LOACH, *who is throwing.*)

LOACH: I'm trying to throw these dice.

BARNET: What I really meant with this fellow Nash, this teacher, was everyone knew but him that he was as queer as a plasticine starting-handle.
(BARNET *goes aside.*)
Ted!

LOACH: Hello?
(BARNET *signals and* LOACH *goes to him.* BARNET *shows him a quarter bottle of spirits.*)

BARNET: Drop of Gordon's? Set you up again.
(LOACH *looks nervously towards* ASH.)

LOACH: I've been off it some time now.

ASH: Old Kent Road, friend. And two hundred for passing Go.

BARNET: D'you want it or don't you?

LOACH: I'm trying to pack it in, aren't I?

ASH: I told you, Ted, we pool our resources we'll be in Easy Street.

BARNET (*putting gin away*): Please yourself.
(LOACH *goes back to game.* BARNET *comes downstage, speaks to* AUDIENCE.)
You can't help some people. I'll think I'll sort the linen, have a smoke . . .
(SISTER *comes on from left with* NURSES.)

SISTER: Mister Barnet——

BARNET: Ah, Sister?

SISTER: Accident case coming up.

BARNET: Right away, Sister.
(*Goes off down front stairs.*)

LOACH: I thought it was for me.

SISTER: Games away now, gentlemen. Mister Flagg, you're due in physio.

100

(*The patients pack the game away.* MICHAEL *and the* PRINCE *bring a stretcher up the stairs.*)

BARNET: Hey. It's young Kenny. Remember him?

They take it across and off left. NURSES *follow. The patients look at the bandaged figure being wheeled by. Flurry of* NURSES *coming and going. Cardiac arrest trolley wheeled across again as* FLAGG *makes his way off right.* BARNET *comes back from left.*)

ASH: By George, no! (*to* LOACH.) You didn't know young Kenneth. Motor bike mad.

(LOACH *wheels game trolley off to the right.* ASH *gets back into bed.* DOCTORS *and* NURSES *continue crossing as lights go down.*)

SCENE SEVEN

BARNET *comes down and into spot.*

BARNET: I could bite my tongue off. Wishing for excitement. Still, that's life, isn't it, madam? That's human nature. We're all of us poised on a knife-edge between the urge for security and a craving for excitement. But you haven't come here to listen to philosophical speculation, you want the facts.

Young Kenneth swerved to avoid a dog, a coach driver swerved to avoid *him*, and went head-on into another coach, killing or maiming sixty passengers. But when I add that one was a party of mongols and the other an old-age pensioners' outing, you'll surely agree that one can sometimes discern A Grand Design. The Great Reaper certainly seems on occasion to have his head screwed on. (*Glances at the screens.*) Casualty's jammed solid, which is why they've brought him

101

here so prompt.

(*Goes towards left and his covered wagon is rolled to him.*
SWEET *comes on from right.*)

SWEET: Where are you going with that?

BARNET: Standing by for Kenneth.

SWEET: It won't be needed.

BARNET: Have they pulled him through?

SWEET: It looks like it.

BARNET: He must have nine lives.

(DOCTORS *return from* KEN'S *bedspace with their machines.*
SWEET *smiles and goes towards left.*)

Go on, run!

(SWEET *turns, comes back.*)

SWEET: I beg your pardon?

BARNET: You're all of a flutter. Say you're not.

SWEET: Why should I be?

BARNET: After some of those noises used to come from the
screens——

SWEET (*delighted*): I beg your pardon——?

BARNET: —when you were giving him a bed-bath.

SWEET: I didn't hear that remark.

(*Goes to help other* NURSES.)

BARNET: Now say there's nothing bent about the healing arts.

(*Turns to push his covered wagon off left.*)

SCENE EIGHT

ASH *alone on stage, in bed. Only* FLAGG'S *and* LOACH'S *remain of
others.* ASH *gets out of bed, puts on slippers and gown as strong
daylight comes on. He gets his basket from his locker. He looks
at the photographs of his son and closes them and puts them out of
sight. Brings his basket down to an armchair. It is a strangely
shaped basket.* ASH *views it miserably and begins work. From the*

left, downstage of the armchairs, KEN *crawls on all fours. His head is still bandaged and he wears gown and slippers. He hides from* ASH *then raises both fists and points his index fingers. He imitates gunfire.*

ASH : Now, Kenny, old son, what are you up to, eh?
(KEN *is now an idiot. His efforts at speech are incoherent but the others are used to his condition and talk over the noise.*)
Come and sit by Uncle Mervyn . . . see what he's doing with his funny old basket. I bet you've never seen a basket that shape. No more have I.
(KEN *laughs at it. He puts it on his head.*)
You could use it for that, I suppose, yes.
(*Laughs and takes it back.* KEN *goes on to stove and begins pretending to shovel coke into the grate.*)
That's right. You like doing that, don't you? Not too much, though, it's warm today.
(FLAGG *comes from the left, now completely recovered and dressed in outdoor clothes.*)

FLAGG : Putting a drop more coal in, Kenny? That's the style then.

ASH : Made your adieus, Mister Flagg?

FLAGG : What's that?

ASH : Said good-bye?

FLAGG : Yes. All this time waiting for the ambulance, I could have been home now, made a cup of tea, if they'd let me walk.

ASH : But after you've been in here some time, the outside world can seem like the headlong rush of the Gadarene swine, they tell me. That's enough, Kenny.
KEN *stops shovelling, turns to listen, sitting on the floor.*)
Besides, you're not as young as you were.

FLAGG : No. (*Yawns, moves about.*) I don't *feel* old.

ASH : That's the style. You're as young as you feel.

FLAGG : Don't feel any older in myself.

103

ASH: But your body's old.

FLAGG: I was thinking this morning . . . Cesar Romero . . . now *he* used to be very young.

ASH: There we are. Tempus fugit.

(KEN *has got an upright chair and straddles it, moving it along and making motor-cycle sounds and actions.* SWEET *comes on right with a simple wooden construction toy.*)

SWEET: Dear me, what a noisy boy you are! And scraping that chair across the floor when it's just been polished, what'll Sister say? Look what nurse has brought. You like these, don't you?

(*He goes down on the floor and begins fitting the pieces together.*)

There's a clever boy!

FLAGG: Any sign of the ambulance, miss?

SWEET: Wherever's the fire, Mr. Flagg? You can't wait to get away from us.

FLAGG: Not that. Only I could have been home . . . had a cup of tea with the old woman . . .

SWEET: All in good time.

FLAGG: Used a toilet with a decent chain . . .

SWEET: How's my basket?

ASH: Nearly done. It's a rather unusual shape.

(SWEET *looks at it and laughs.*)

SWEET: It looks like one of those old-fashioned corsets.

(*Goes off, left.* ASH *looks after her without smiling. He puts the basket aside.*)

ASH: How are you getting on, young Kenny? Uncle Mervyn give a hand? Now here's a funny piece. Where d'you think that perisher goes, eh?

(BARNET *comes from right with* ORDERLY.)

BARNET: That one and that one, out. All right, Princess?

(*They clear Bed 3.* BARNET *drifts away and the* ORDERLY *gets on with it.*)

I suppose young Ken arouses your old interest in boys?

ASH: Once a teacher, always a teacher, eh, Kenny?

104

BARNET: He's going to need some teaching and all, wher*ever* they put him.

ASH: And since society sees fit to condemn me to a life of clerical drudgery, I shall do whatever I can to help him. (LOACH *drifts on from the side, dressed for the outside world.*)

BARNET: This your basket, Cinders?

ASH: I hope you're not about to criticize that basket. I've had about all I can stand in that direction. The perishing thing's been like a reproach every day of my confinement, staring me in the face saying: "Well, Clever Dick?"

LOACH: Same with me, me old mate, never any use with my hands . . .

ASH: But I *had* a use. I had gifts. Small gifts, which I offered humbly to the world and only asked that I be let use them. Why should I spend my life doing the very things I'm least suited for?

BARNET: Very good. Better than the telly.
(*The* ORDERLY *has cleared the beds.* BARNET *rejoins him.*)
Well done, sir. Let's go and sort the linen. Ted!
(LOACH *goes to him.* BARNET *gives him a small bottle.*)
Don't let anyone see it, all right?

LOACH: What do I owe you?

BARNET: With the money for the gee-gees, say two quid and we'll call it square.

LOACH: How's it come to two quid?

BARNET: I've got my overheads to cover.
(*Takes notes from* LOACH *and goes off, right.* LOACH *swigs.* KEN *crawls to him, pretends to shoot him, grabs his legs.*)

LOACH: That's right, Kenny, me old mate. You shoot me dead. I'd appreciate that. The prospect I got. Great barn of a place, miles from fucking civilization.

ASH: Don't use words like that. In front of the boy.

LOACH: He ain't a boy. He's a grown man.

ASH: What do you know about it?
(LOACH *moves again, towards* FLAGG.)

105

LOACH: We got the same ambulance, eh, Dad?

FLAGG: When it comes.

LOACH: Marvellous, isn't it? Nationalization.

FLAGG: I could have been home in ten minutes. On the bus.

LOACH: Where's that?

FLAGG: Islington.

LOACH: Very nice.

FLAGG: Used to be beautiful there. Before the Agricultural Hall was sold to the corporation.

LOACH: There you are.

FLAGG: Used to have Market Garden Week there . . . Dairy Week . . .

(LOACH *winces, rubs leg*.)

LOACH: Jesus God Al-bleeding-mighty. Humorous really, when you think of me out India way. Or Africa. Malaya . . . my own bearer . . . fifty wogs under me . . . I was a sahib.

(TYLER *goes across, carried by the black* ORDERLY. *He seems dwarfish and helpless*.)

TYLER: How are you, Kenny, smiling through?

(*And they all make cheering noises as he exits*.)

ASH: Wonderful spirit.

(LAKE *has come on too*.)

LAKE: Ready, these patients? Ambulance for you now. Mister—eh—(*looks at her list*.) Flagg and Mister Loach. That you?

FLAGG: That's right, miss.

LOACH: Here it is then. No going back now.

FLAGG: I had a bag.

LAKE: Here.

FLAGG: Cheerio, then, all.

(*Shakes hands with* ASH, *while* LOACH *goes to the left*.)

LOACH (*shouts off*): Cheero, me old mates.

(*A feeble cheer off*.)

ASH: Don't let me see you in here again.

FLAGG: No fear.

(KEN *hugs* FLAGG's *legs*.)

ASH: All right, Kenny.

(FLAGG *goes to the stairs with* LAKE. *She helps him descend out of sight.* LOACH *shakes with* ASH.)

LOACH: Cheerio, Cambridge. If you feel like dropping in sometime, I say, there's a Green Line bus not far off.

ASH: I'll see what I can do, yes. And good luck.

LOACH: And you're going to ask your landlady about the room?

ASH: Well, I think it's probably gone, as a matter of fact, but——

LOACH: You can ask.

ASH: Yes.

(KEN *hugs his legs*.)

LOACH: Bye-bye, Kenny. Well. Now. Where's old Blackie gone?

(*Goes off down the stairs after* LAKE. KEN *goes on with his toy.* ASH *looks at the ward, only his bed remains. He goes back to* KEN *and sits on the floor*.)

ASH: D'you know, son, we speak the most beautiful language in the world? That's our heritage. The tongue that Shakespeare spake. Yet most of the people you meet can utter nothing better than a stream of filth. I'm not sorry to see him go. I mean, I did my best, but he clung like a limpet. Mind you, I think one should be able to mix without actually lowering standards. Like the time I took my slum boys camping.

(KEN *laughs*, ASH *ruffles his hair*.)

Yes, I did. What's more, I tried an experiment. Paired them off with college boys. Nicely spoken lads, you know. And the ragamuffins visibly *rose*, they actually raised themselves. But—this is the crux of the matter, son— the college lads were totally unscathed. And that's the secret of the governing class. The secret of the Royal Family.

(KEN *has finished the puzzle.*)

Clever boy, there's a clever boy.

(KEN *laughs, breaks it up.*)

And when I was a teacher I was privileged to know
many of the Royal Family personally. No side at all.
Regal bearing, yes, but not the snobbery of the newly
rich. Simple dignity. Which is what is missing from so
much of life today. Grace. Style. We're all the same,
we need something fine to which to aspire. We want to
rise, not sink in the bog.

(KEN *makes signs that he wants* ASH *to help him again.
Together they begin to assemble the toy.*)

My hat, the old Queen! She'd come inspecting. We'd
spit-and-polish everywhere. Gym, library, canteen, even
the toilets. Know what she'd ask to see? The brush
cupboards.

(*Laugh at the recollection.* KEN *laughs at his laughter.*)

ASH: There isn't nearly enough of that sort of spirit about
these days.

(*They go on working.*)

SCENE NINE

*Music, lights and a pantomime transformation. Stained glass
in the Gothic windows, church bells and a wedding march.*

*A carpeted staircase comes down centre and two bridal pairs
appear—Boyd and Sister McPhee, Neil and Staff Nurse Norton,
the grooms in kilts, the brides in white.*

*The patients, quick and dead, appear with the nursing staff from
both sides, throwing confetti, streamers, rice, and waving Union
Jacks.*

*The Chaplain comes up the front steps, now a bishop, mitred
and golden. An acolyte bears his train.*

Matron calls for cheers, which are given by the whole company to the bridal group as they shake hands with the chaplain. The acolyte turns to us and we see that he is Barnet in black-face.

BARNET: It's a funny old world we live in and you're lucky to get out of it alive.
A black-face band marches on playing a cakewalk and BARNET *joins them with a tambourine or banjo. At once the whole company dance to the music.*

CURTAIN

Curtain rises and dance continues. Each group comes down to bow: bridal quartet first, next nursing staff, then patients. Music and dance stop suddenly. A silent tableau, the patients frozen in their attitudes.

CURTAIN